B[

Conversations

The Entertaining Dialogue of Pet Rabbits

Includes Best Care Practices
And Tips For Pet Rabbit Owners

Jana Brock

Co-Authored by *"The Littles"*

Jana Brock

Published by Starry Night Publishing.Com

Rochester, New York

Copyright 2017 Jana Brock

Disclaimer

This book was written with house rabbit owners in mind, those who might want to get one in the future and people who want to learn some basics of care. It is also a good resource for bunny sitters, especially those who do not have a great deal of hands-on experience with rabbit care and handling.

The author is not a veterinarian, but rather an adept researcher, pet rabbit owner and caretaker for other rabbits. She does not support rabbits being used for the fur or clothing industry, cosmetics other harmful or potentially harmful research and/or testing, any activity where the rabbit is at risk for injury or stress, or animal abuse, cruelty or neglect. This book is in support of responsible and compassionate pet ownership.

This information is not intended to solely address one rabbit breed, though much of it is based on average-sized rabbits such as Mini Lops and the smaller Holland Lop house rabbits.

Regardless the breed of your rabbit, this information is not intended to replace what you can find in a more comprehensive rabbit care book or credible website. It is also not intended to replace the advice of an experienced, *rabbit-savvy* (someone who has a lot of experience specifically with rabbits) veterinarian. Some information in this book was written strictly for entertainment purposes.

If you have a pet rabbit that requires specialty care or has special needs, you should research additional information, consult with a qualified veterinarian or talk with rabbit experts who have hands-on experience with your situation.

Many aspects of pet rabbits are still understudied in the United States and elsewhere. For this reason, the term "expert" is used somewhat loosely. Information shared publicly about pet rabbit care and ownership can vary greatly, be conflicting, inaccurate, misinterpreted, misunderstood and be taken out of context.

Since information and opinions can vary, readers must educate themselves and use good judgment when making decisions about their rabbit. None of the information in this book should be construed, or perceived, as advice.

When addressing topics that have inherent conflict or when addressing information where there is some disagreement among experts and experienced rabbit owners, the author typically defers to nature and what it intended for rabbits.

If you have an emergency with your rabbit, see a veterinarian immediately. It is important to find one that has a *comprehensive understanding of and experience* and stays current with science, treatment and training specific to these animals.

Dedication

Dedicated to Alexis. She has encountered everything from predator sharks to land beasts without so much as a flinch. When asked if she knew why wild and domesticated animals are drawn to her, she said that everything in nature has its own way of communicating. She is just willing to listen.

Jana Brock

For ease of writing, the author uses "he" or "him"
when referring to rabbits. The information in this book pertains to
both males (bucks) and females (does).

Jana Brock

Contents

Jana Brock

Preface

Like other animals, rabbits have their own way of speaking. It is a rabbit language, of sorts. Since they are considered prey, rabbits are among the quietest animals in nature. Deciphering what they say can be tricky. I had to become a very good listener. It also helps to have a good imagination.

Bunny Conversations is my light-hearted documentation of endearing discussions which occur primarily between Lila and Bandit. I affectionately refer to them as *The Littles*.

These two young Holland Lops came into my life when they were both kits, just 8 and 12 weeks old. They were not my first pet rabbits and I am sure they won't be my last.

Lila is a well-behaved doe. She weighs just over 2.5 pounds and has a sweet disposition. Bandit is a tad smaller but has a very large personality - a somewhat mischievous and overly-confident buck.

Typical for house rabbits, they were guarded when they first arrived. I respected their space and quickly earned their trust. They now refer to me as their *Huma*, which is short for *Human Ma* (their words, not mine).

The Littles need things to be a certain way in their living environment. They also need socialization. In addition to consistent contact with humans, they have safe interactions with visiting rabbits – some I bunny sit and others that arrive in need of rehabilitation and rehoming (rescues).

I hope you find this information helpful as well as amusing. Thank you for reading this book and, as always, thank you for caring!

Jana Brock

Chapter One
The Littles

Bandit: Hey, Lila. Want some popcorn?
Lila: Huma says we can't have popcorn.
Bandit: Why not? It smells delicious.
Lila: She said we would never eat it if we lived out in nature.
Bandit: We could just find a big popcorn field.
Lila: You are thinking of corn on the cob.
Bandit: Oh. Well, let's ask for some of that.
Lila: We can't have any corn. It's not good for rabbits.
Bandit: There sure are a lot of things we can't eat.
Lila: Yup.
Bandit: Thinking about it makes me hungry.
Lila: Go back to sleep, Bandit.

Lila: Did you hear that?
Bandit: Hear what?
Lila: I think I heard a clown.
Bandit: What is a clown?
Lila: A very dangerous monster. Even humans are afraid of them.
Bandit: Why?
Lila: Some clowns hurt people.
Bandit: Will they hurt us too?
Lila: They steal baby rabbits.
Bandit: Oh no. Clowns are terrifying!
(I come in the room)
Me: Hi Littles. What are you doing?
Bandit & Lila: We heard a clown!
Me: That was just the television. Are you two afraid of clowns?
Bandit: (standing taller) Lila is, but don't worry. I told her I would protect her.
Lila: Are you serious right now?

Bandit: Lila, don't just stand there. Help me dig.
Lila: I like playing in our camping enclosure.
Bandit: Don't you want to see what's on the other side of this fence?
There is a whole world out there just waiting to be discovered.
Lila: A big world with predators. Don't you remember Huma
protecting us from those racoons yesterday?
Bandit: I could have protected us.
Lila: You weigh a pound-and-a-half.
Bandit: True, but I know karate.
Lila: You don't know karate.
Bandit: Well, I want to learn it.
Lila: Cover up that hole, half-pint. We aren't going anywhere.

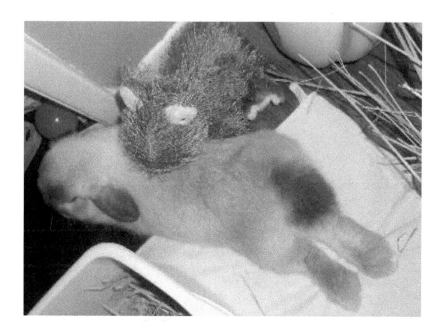

Me: Lila, are you comfortable with Froggy there?

Lila: Not really, but he won't move. I asked him several times.

Me: Froggy is just a stuffed animal. He can't talk or hear like you and Bandit can.

Lila: What? Why would you stuff a frog? That is horrible.

Me: No. I mean - he is just a pretend frog. He's not real.

Lila: What do you mean he is not real? He's right beside me.

Me: Yes, he is there. I just meant that Froggy is a toy. He was never a real frog.

Lila: You keep saying he's not real.

Me: Some things about life are confusing.

Lila: Especially frogs.

Lila: I'm bored. Wanna go play in the tunnel?
Bandit: I am trying to sleep.
Lila: You always sleep.
Bandit: You are a month older than me and way bigger. I need more rest than you do.
Lila: I'm not much bigger than you.
Bandit: Seriously - you are huge. What do you weigh now, two pounds?
Lila: I'm just big-boned.
Bandit: Yeah, right.
Lila: If you are going to be rude, I'll go play without you.
Bandit: You could use the exercise.
Lila: Don't push it, short stuff.

I sensed something was going on with The Littles. When I asked Lila what happened, she told me Bandit wouldn't stop chasing her. Even when she asked nicely, he just kept doing it until she was exhausted. She has decided not to speak to him for at least two minutes. She is sure that will teach him a meaningful lesson.

Bandit: Lila, what is this shiny thing?
Lila: A refrigerator.
Bandit: There is a black and white bunny in there. He keeps staring at me. It's creeping me out.
Lila: Oh, Bandit. You are imagining things.
Bandit: Look for yourself.
Lila: (She sees her reflection) Oh, my goodness. I see one that looks just like me. What is happening here?
Bandit: I don't know, but I hope they're not clowns!
Lila: I'm sure there is a good explanation. Besides, Huma told us there are no clowns in the house. Remember?
Bandit: Well, they managed to get in somehow. What if they escape from the refrigerator and steal us?
Lila: I don't think that's possible.
Bandit: It could happen.

Jana Brock

Chapter Two
Pet Rabbit Expense

Bandit: Huma, today is my birthday. Where is my raisin?
Me: I'm sorry, Bandit. You are too young for raisins.
Bandit: I'm 4 months old. That's almost an adult.
Me: You barely weigh 2 pounds.
Bandit: Lila gets raisins.
Me: She is one month older than you.
Bandit: This is discrimination.
Me: It is not discrimination. Next week I will give you half of a raisin. I want to make sure your digestive system handles it okay.
Bandit: My what?
Me: Your tummy.
Bandit: Can you at least give Lila a raisin?
Me: Will you steal it from her?
Bandit: It's not stealing. It's helping.
Me: No, but nice try.
Bandit: Sigh…

House rabbits are referred to as pets, domesticated rabbits or companions. Though "companion" has taken on a specific meaning in other contexts, here it simply refers to a pet.

Domesticated rabbits can be wonderful companions. They are cute, lovable and amusing. Like most animals, they have varying personalities. In a good environment where they are properly cared for, rabbits can bond with humans and other pets.

At face value, a house rabbit seems like the perfect companion for everyone. For people who can commit to proper care and handling, this is true. However, anyone looking for a low-maintenance, easy-to-care-for pet should not get one.

Unlike some animals, studies which are specific to domesticated rabbits are somewhat lacking. Also, there are still not many rabbit-specialty programs in veterinary schools. Rather, rabbits are lumped into the exotic pet category.

Hopefully, rabbits will have their own category (separate from "exotic pets") in the future. Until then, a great deal can be learned about best care practices from information made available by experienced owners, rabbit-savvy veterinarians and house rabbit organizations.

Whether you already have a pet rabbit or would like to get one, it is important to educate yourself and your family on the pros and cons of having one in your home. Providing a good environment goes beyond basic feeding, veterinarian costs and the rabbit-human interaction.

A pet rabbit's life in captivity should be a long, happy journey. When responsibly cared for and barring any serious problems, they can live ten years or more. Rabbit ownership is a big commitment that should not be taken lightly.

The next few chapters contain information that rabbit owners need to know. It is not intended to discourage you or your family from adopting a pet rabbit. Rather, it is to share realities of rabbit ownership, lessons learned, tips and tricks and best care practices.

Pet rabbits need humans who are willing to learn as much as possible. Knowledge is also important because far too many animals are mistreated, abandoned or euthanized. The more we learn, the more these problems can be avoided.

Bandit: What is Huma doing with this sweepy thing?
Lila: I'm not sure. Huma, what are you doing with this sweepy thing?
Me: I am cleaning.
Lila: (looking at Bandit) She is cleaning.
Bandit: Do you know how much time it takes to mark everything? You know, her territory. My territory…
Me: Looks like a lot of work.
Bandit: Then why are you cleaning it up?
Me: Your primary living space needs to be sanitary.
Bandit: It's sanitary enough for me.
Me: Leaving poops on the floor is not sanitary. You are both litter box trained. From now on, just go potty where you are supposed to.
Bandit: If I do that, how will Lila know which areas belong to me?
Me: You have a shared living space. There is no reason to mark your territory.
Bandit: It's like you don't know me at all.

Pet rabbit expenses can vary greatly. Hay, food and other basic supplies will need to be purchased on a regular basis. In addition to what you will buy for day-to-day care, you will likely have unexpected or emergency costs. Veterinary expenses to treat injuries or illness can quickly exceed budgets of the unprepared.

Money Realities

Adopting rabbits (rather than buying them) helps with overpopulation. That, in turn, helps decrease the number of rabbits that are abandoned to shelters. Though not always possible, adopting is highly encouraged among experienced rabbit owners.

If you do not have a shelter or rescue facility near you, it is helpful to check the local newspapers for online ads. Often, people use ads to help rehome domesticated rabbits.

When adopting from a shelter or other rescue facility, it is not uncommon to pay a small fee to pick up your new cutie. This fee helps shelters continue providing their vital services of rehabilitation and rehoming of unwanted pets. It also ensures that rabbits are not acquired by people who do not have good intentions for them.

If you buy from a breeder, you might pay $50-$250, though purchase prices could be higher. In this situation, it is not uncommon to get an animal that has not been altered (spayed or neutered). That means you will also have to pay a rabbit-savvy veterinarian to perform an alteration surgery which will be an additional $140-$250 (or more).

In addition to basic veterinary expenses, domesticated rabbits require supplies which must be refreshed on a regular basis. At the very least, your rabbit should have a sizeable crate or primary rabbit house, litter box, a supply of safe litter material, high quality food pellets (if used), water bottle, food dish, plenty of hay, fresh rabbit-safe vegetables and a hay feeder (container).

Rabbits also require safe wood to chew on, pet fencing (or pet playpen materials), cord wrap (cord protector), carpeting strips or floor mats, carboard boxes (clean – no tape or accessible glue), nail clippers, a brush and rabbit-safe toys.

Since bunnies are fragile creatures, their health can change in a matter of hours. For this reason, many rabbit owners have a basic rabbit emergency care pack. This topic is discussed more in a later chapter.

Purchasing what you need for your rabbit could be expensive, or not. It depends upon the item, whether it is easy to get in your location and other factors.

In addition to the basics, rabbit owners should plan on saving some money for emergency veterinary appointments. Unexpected treatment costs for these animals are quite common.

Jana Brock

Chapter Three
Family Considerations

Bandit: Lila, do you ever think about living outdoors?
Lila: Not really.
Bandit: I heard the humans talking about wild rabbits. I bet they find a lot of treats outside.
Lila: Maybe, but rabbits are prey animals. The ones in the wild don't live very long.
Bandit: What is a prey animal?
Lila: They get eaten by other animals.
Bandit: Are you serious?
Lila: I'm afraid so.
Bandit: That is outrageous!
Lila: And terrifying.
Bandit: Thank goodness I have karate skills. Predators won't come near us. Not if they are smart, anyway.
Lila: How reassuring.

Most people consider their pets part of the family. Since rabbits are social creatures, they need frequent interaction with their humans. To avoid problems, consideration should be given to the needs of everyone.

Other Family Members

Since a rabbit's main source of food is hay and dried grasses, it is important to know whether anyone in your home has hay or grass-related allergies. Also, think about family members with pet allergies. Some people tolerate rabbits and some become symptomatic around them.

Most people today realize that small children and rabbits do not mix. There must be very close supervision if you have a youngster. Children can be harmed by the rabbit, and vice versa. The topic of young children and rabbits is discussed in more detail later.

Careful thought must also be given to pets you already have. Since rabbits are prey animals they are easily frightened. Many have met an untimely death when other animals have been improperly introduced or mistakenly trusted with rabbits. Incorporating new pets into the house requires wisdom, patience, time and vigilant supervision.

Keep in mind that rabbits do not do well with abrupt, loud noises. Historically, the topic of a rabbit's fragile heart was somewhat challenged. Today, we know that rabbits can literally be scared to death.

Consider the needs of all existing family members before getting a house rabbit. Consider the needs of the rabbit, too. Bringing one into a new environment is already stressful for them. It would create further stress if they had to be rehomed elsewhere because your environment turned out to be unsuitable.

Changing Your Home

Are you willing to change your family home to accommodate a pet rabbit? If so, great! If not, a pet rabbit might not be the right pet for you and your family.

Though rabbits are immensely entertaining, they are also destructive by nature. Significant damage can occur in a short amount of time if chewable items are not protected or placed out of reach. In fact, destruction of household items is so common with pet rabbits that it is referred to as *bunstruction*.

There is a lot you can do to protect your space. If you do not do so, a rabbit can peel (and often, eat) wallpaper, wall paint, stucco, baseboards, molding, sheetrock, décor, cords, toxic plants, furniture legs and other home items.

Eating household items can, and most likely will, cause illness, intestinal blockages or develop other problems which could be fatal. These problems are easily overcome by properly rabbit-proofing your living space (discussed later).

Jana Brock

Chapter Four
Bunny Sitters

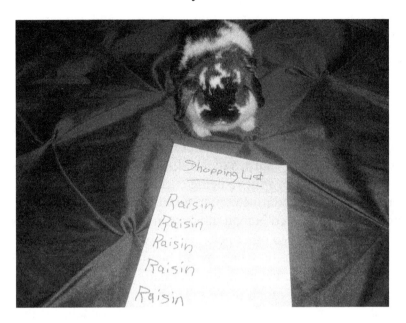

Bandit: Where are you going, Huma?
Me: To the store. I'll be right back.
Bandit: Oh, hey - can you pick some things up for me and Lila?
Me: Sure. What do you need?
Bandit: I have a list. Here you go…
Me: Bandit, this just has the word raisin written over and over.
Bandit: Yup. I thought it would help you remember.
Me: How very thoughtful. Thank you.
Bandit: No problem.

You want to go on vacation but cannot leave your rabbit unattended even for one night. You need a rabbit-savvy pet boarding facility. For most rabbit owners, this presents a problem.

Many pet care facilities will not accept house rabbits. Most do not have enough experience with proper care and handling, nor do they have the appropriate space to house them. Since rabbits are fragile, leaving them in that type of boarding facility is risky.

Considerations

Leaving your rabbit in an unsuitable environment even for a day or two could cause problems, including exposure to fleas or ticks; development of snuffles (cold-like symptoms) or other serious illness; fear and anxiety due to being caged near barking dogs or other noisy animals; confinement to a small cage with no regular exercise; lack of trusted human interaction and a myriad of issues which may not apply to other pets.

Could you just fix whatever problem arises after you return? That depends. Something as simple as treating fleas is often a complex problem for rabbit owners. Many normal-for-other-pet medications or treatments are not good for these animals due to their sensitive systems and thin, fragile skin.

Your extended absence could also cause your pet rabbit to enter a depressive state where he stops eating and drinking. From there, a series of cascading events occur and the animal could suffer a rapid health decline.

Some veterinarian clinics will board your rabbit for you. However, close attention should be given to the available accommodations.

Your rabbit would likely be placed in a small cage within earshot of loud animals that scare him. Veterinarians and their staff also have busy schedules which makes it difficult to provide boarded rabbits with enough exercise, play time and attention. Finally, the cost of veterinary clinic boarding is typically high.

It may sound as though there is no solution for the lack of rabbit-savvy boarding facilities. However, all these problems can be overcome by either finding someone nearby who is experienced with pet rabbits or training someone to bunny sit for you.

Training a Bunny Sitter

Though this book has a great deal that is entertaining, one of the reasons it has been written is to help people understand the basics of rabbit care and handling.

Consider loaning this book to your prospective bunny sitter. It is a quick read and can help immensely. If there is something you do differently than what is published here, be sure to inform them so that they stay in alignment with your routines.

People generally like house rabbits. For that reason, it might be easy to find someone to help. Have a discussion with your prospective sitter to see what they know before you begin the training process. Since there are so many historic teachings that do not align with proper care, it is helpful to let them know that many misunderstandings exist.

Show your sitter how to properly handle your pet. Part of your training might be to tell the sitter not to pick up or carry the rabbit unless it is necessary. This will greatly decrease the chances of injury and help minimize your pet's stress level.

Taking your rabbit to the sitter's home will require some additional discussion about safety. He should not be able to access electrical cords or other household items that might be dangerous. Even if your rabbit has free roam of your house, it is best to limit his living space in an unfamiliar environment. Of course, he should still be allowed a large area to exercise several times each day.

Write down the foods your rabbit eats, what amounts he should be given and at what times. Stress that no new foods should be added to his diet while you are away - not even in small amounts.

Teach the sitter about litter box maintenance and the importance of keeping everything as clean as possible. Explain why it is necessary to monitor the rabbit's waste (poops).

It is also important that your sitter monitor eating and drinking to avoid digestive problems and dehydration. Provide your veterinarian's information so that if any problems arise, the sitter can call for advice and, if necessary, get rapid care.

Make sure that no other animals are present that could scare or harm your pet rabbit. Since he is not bonded with them, they should not have direct contact.

Also, talk to your bunny sitter about the dangers of your rabbit hearing loud noises such as barking dogs or anything else that might startle or scare him. Being in an unfamiliar environment is stressful enough without these added problems.

Training a friend, family member or neighbor prior to your departure is extremely beneficial. It will greatly reduce your worry and minimize the stress your absence creates for your rabbit.

Chapter Five
Rabbits As Gifts

Lila & Bandit: Oh, hey Huma….

Me: Hello, Littles. What are you doing?

Lila: Dancing.

Me: I did not know rabbits could dance.

Lila: Yup, we dance. Mostly at night when you are asleep. Bandit has been teaching me some new moves.

Bandit: Show her your twerk, Lila.

Me: Wait….what? No! Absolutely no twerking. Rabbits do not twerk.

Lila: Why not?

Me: Twerking is very inappropriate, especially for rabbits your age.

Bandit: Well, the human on TV said it's fun and it's sexy.

Me: Alright, that's enough of that kind of talk.

Bandit: What did I say wrong?

Me: Sexy is not a good word to use.

Bandit: So, no more twerking and no more sexy?

Me: That is correct. And definitely no more television!

In comparison with other pets, rabbit-specific studies are somewhat lacking. However, some studies have shown that rabbits are the third most commonly surrendered animals living in shelters and other rescue facilities. Cats and dogs occupy the number one and two spots.

When animals are not adopted into forever homes, they are euthanized (killed). This fate of death can be avoided by ethical breeding, knowing the realities of these animals prior to getting one and learning the basics of best care practices.

Young Children and Rabbits

Historically, rabbits were believed to be appropriate gifts for children at Easter time. Many of those rabbits were abandoned, rehomed or died very young. Thanks to the efforts of responsible rabbit owners and pet organizations who raise awareness about rabbit care, the practice of using rabbits as gifts has decreased.

Though exceptions exist, rabbits are generally not good gifts for young children, regardless the occasion. Young children are not yet old enough, nor responsible enough, to understand proper rabbit handling and care. They also do not realize the harm they can inadvertently do.

Mishandling a rabbit causes him to become injured. It also increases his mistrust of humans. Since rabbits are hardwired to be silent when they are sick or hurt, inexperienced rabbit owners often have no idea the animal needs medical help.

Children can also get hurt. When rabbits are mishandled or become frightened, they will respond by scratching or biting. This is instinctual behavior and not the fault of the animal. Rabbits will do whatever possible to get away when they do not feel safe.

It is not realistic to expect any animal to sit quietly and tolerate mistreatment or mishandling, however unintentional. Even so, that is sometimes the expectation of inexperienced owners.

Often, when the rabbit reacts to improper handling, it is automatically considered a problem pet. It is then tossed into a cage until it can be removed from the home.

Parents who want to get a pet rabbit for young children must be willing to fully accept day-to-day responsibilities for proper care, handling, expense and the long-term commitment. They must also closely supervise all interactions between the animal and young children.

If parents are not interested in having their own house rabbit and accepting all responsibilities that come with proper care, they should not get one. Instead, they could buy their child a stuff animal, a chocolate bunny or some other gift.

By purchasing a more age-appropriate gift, no children will be scratched or bitten. Additionally, the rabbit will have a chance at finding a forever home. This will avoid the animal being harmed, neglected, abandoned or unnecessarily euthanized.

Jana Brock

Chapter Six
Ca-Yute!

Me: Hi Littles. What's up?
Bandit: I'm just chillin'. You know how it is.
Me: I see. Lila, what are you looking at?
Lila: That chewed spot on the wall.
Me: Bandit, do you know anything about that?
Bandit: I started to fix it. I'm not finished yet.
Me. Bunstruction project?
Bandit: Yup.
Me: I appreciate it, but that wall doesn't really need to be fixed.
Bandit: Are you sure? I don't mind.
Me: I am quite sure. Thank you, though.
Bandit: Anytime, Huma. Anytime.

Pet rabbits are cute, no doubt. Baby rabbits (called *kits* or *kittens*) are so cute, in fact, that many people find them irresistible. It is no wonder that so many have found their way into the homes of unprepared humans.

Rapid Growth

The reality of rabbit kits is different than most people think. In fact, the adorable baby rabbit stage is very short-lived. In a matter of months, the baby look is gone and a more mature looking rabbit emerges. Once that happens, people who acquired their rabbit because of cuteness often lose interest.

As a rabbit approaches adulthood, his behavior also changes. Prior to young rabbits being altered and before they are even fully grown, the teen-stage hormones begin to surge. This causes undesirable behaviors to rapidly increase.

For experienced owners who understand hormone-driven behavior, this is not a problem. Others might think their once-cute rabbit is now the worst pet ever, and out the door it goes.

Unwanted pet rabbits that are not responsibly rehomed often die within their first year of life. This can be caused by mishandling, poor diet, outright neglect, improper veterinary care (overmedicating or giving the animal the wrong procedures, treatments or medications), constant confinement (over caging) or otherwise.

Prior to getting a pet rabbit, consider visiting a place where you can interact with and observe their in-captivity behavior. People who work at pet shelters or have rescues are often willing to help newcomers by talking about rabbit ownership pros and cons.

Also, there are plenty of credible websites and videos which are provided by house rabbit owners who freely share good information. Arming yourself with the realities of rabbit ownership will ensure you make a good decision about whether one of these animals is the right pet for you.

Happy Rabbit Tip

Age of Rabbit	Life Stage Category
0 to 4 months	Kit or Kitten (baby)
4 to 6 months	Adolescent, Teen or Teenager
7 months to 1 year	Young Adult
1 year to 5 years	Mature Adult
5-6 years and older	Senior

LoveYourRabbit.com

Note: Age breaks and life stage category terms may vary depending upon information source

Knowing the life stage of your rabbit is important. Among other things, his age gives you a guideline of what foods, and how much of those foods, to feed him. His age will also determine other factors involved with proper care.

Like much of the distributed information about these animals, age categorizations and the verbiage related to it can vary depending upon the information source. For example, the adolescent or teen stage is sometimes included in either the baby category or the young adult.

Jana Brock

Chapter Seven
Older Children

Lila: Huma, I need to talk to you while Bandit is asleep.
Me: Sure, Lila. What is going on?
Lila: He really wants a raisin.
Me: I know, but he has another week or so before his system is ready.
Lila: Okay. Can I have a raisin tonight?
Me: Did Bandit put you up to this?
Lila: Uhhhhhh….
Me: Good talk, Lila.
Lila: Is that a no?
Me: That's a no.

Preteen and teenage pet owners are prevalent on social media sites. An impressively high number of them seem to handle their responsibilities well. Others would make any responsible rabbit owner want to reach right through the internet and rescue their animal.

Whether you are planning to bring a rabbit home for your teen/preteen or you already have done so, it is important to closely supervise the pet care process - at least initially. Learning about proper care and handling of pet rabbits will ensure the animal has a healthy environment and a happy life.

It is important to make sure your teen/preteen learns what he or she needs to know. Making these preparations will help your child be a good rabbit owner and give you peace of mind.

Dolly's Commitment to Proper Care

It is encouraging to witness kids who take their pet ownership responsibilities seriously. Typically, success stories are the result of parents placing proper care and handling as a priority not only for themselves, but for all family members.

Dolly is a young girl who actively participates in one of the rabbit groups on social media. She proved that kids are perfectly capable of properly caring for pet rabbits when they are committed to the process.

This young rabbit owner has two bunnies – a bonded pair. Her parents had agreed to allow her to have house rabbits if she completed an online pet rabbit care course. After Dolly completed the course, she took it upon herself to continue learning.

Not only did Dolly post pictures and videos on social media showing two healthy, happy rabbits, but she was always eager to help new rabbit owners when they had questions. When asked by another online rabbit owner what her age was, Dolly humbly stated that she was 13 years old.

Chapter Eight
Bonding With Your Rabbit

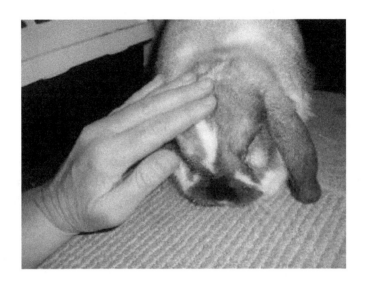

Bandit: Who is Huma petting?
Lila: That is Jo. She is staying here this week.
Bandit: Why?
Lila: Her humans are on vacation so we are bunny sitting.
Bandit: Why isn't she staying with us in our room?
Lila: Jo isn't used to being around other rabbits. It might not be safe.
Bandit: I won't hurt her.
Lila: She is about four times bigger than we are, so…
Bandit: That doesn't matter.
Lila: We also haven't been properly bonded with her yet.
Bandit: Jo has probably heard about my karate skills. I bet she is afraid of me.
Lila: Do you really believe that?
Bandit: Word gets around, Lila.

When bringing rabbits into a new environment, they will be cautious and somewhat frightened. It is tempting to pick up a new or visiting rabbit and start passing him around to family members and friends. However, it is important to refrain from doing so.

Forcing pet rabbits into social situations with humans they neither know, nor trust, causes unnecessary anxiety and fear. The same is true of other house pets. Most house rabbits need to go through a proper bonding process with other animals as well as their new humans before they feel comfortable and safe.

Patience is Key

The process of bringing a new rabbit home is stressful for him. He will naturally want to retreat and hide. Your home is unfamiliar territory. Before you acquired him, he may have had bonds with other animals and his prior owner. Those bonds have been abruptly broken.

We are taught to hold human infants and make sure they have plenty of contact with us. Wouldn't that same thing hold true for a new rabbit? Actually, no.

Allowing children or others to shower your new rabbit with attention will only stress him out further. He already has a lot going on and he needs patience and compassion while he adjusts to his new environment.

Resist the urge to handle him, especially at first. He will come to you when he is ready. Rushing the process will only make him more guarded. If he is a very young kit that was handled before you got him, the adjustment should be easier. However, even baby rabbits need time to feel safe in a new home.

It will help to confine your new rabbit's primary space, at least initially. Make sure he has a tunnel or a dark retreat to hide in. Retreats (dark hiding places) are part of a rabbit's nature and should be considered a basic need. This will help him feel safe and secure.

When you feed him, refresh his hay and water or just clean his space, be careful to avoid quick movements. In time, he will sniff around to investigate what you are doing. It is very important that you allow him this opportunity so that he gets comfortable with you being there.

If you plan to expand your new rabbit's space, do it slowly over several weeks. This is especially important if he is very young. A smaller space makes him feel secure and helps establish good litter box habits.

Active Bonding

Human-animal bonding begins once you bring your rabbit home. The very act of allowing him space is helping him trust you. To start a more active bonding process, sit on the floor with your rabbit and allow him to come to you. When he cautiously approaches, do not reach out or pick him up.

A rabbit will use his natural senses to investigate you, especially his sense of smell. You want to let him sniff you so that in the future, he knows you are not a threat. Your rabbit can hear and smell you long before you get close to him.

Most rabbit senses are strong. In fact, they can detect food beneath the ground. They also have excellent vision and hearing. It is said that rabbits can hear subtle sounds that are one-and-a-half to two miles away. The original species (wild rabbits) would not survive long without these abilities.

Even when he is familiar with you, your pet rabbit will likely sniff you and the area around where you are sitting. If you remain still and just allow him time, he should start putting his little paws on you and even climb up on your lap.

Understanding the prey-animal nature of your rabbit is critical, which is why you must never chase him. Prey animals instinctively flee when they are chased by predators. You don't want your animal to view you as a threat. If you chase him, that is exactly what will happen. This makes bonding even more difficult.

Grooming

If you have two or more rabbits that are already bonded, you will see them groom one another's heads and bodies. You will notice that this behavior is comforting to them. Since rabbits are prodigious (exceptional) groomers, self-cleaning is a strong part of their nature.

When your rabbit is comfortable allowing you to do so, bring your hand up to his head from the side so that he can see it. Rabbits have a blind spot in front of their heads. If he all the sudden feels something on his head and did not see it coming, he may be startled and feel unsafe.

Each time you bring your hand to his head, touch it and then slowly withdraw your hand. Repeat that process a few times before petting his head, if he allows you to do so. You want him to know that your approaching hand is not a threat to him.

This slow hand-to-head process is especially important if you have a rescued rabbit that may not be used to human contact. Sadly, some rabbits come from humans who were unkind, neglectful or even abusive. Those rabbits will often be more fearful and mistrusting, which is understandable.

Forcing a relationship with an animal that was mistreated, neglected or even abused prior to coming home with you will not be in your best interest, nor his. It may take a long time (weeks or even months) of patience and bonding practice before he trusts you.

If a rabbit's body language tells you that he is not comfortable with you petting him yet, respect his wishes. Just sit quietly beside him and let him continue to investigate each time you interact.

In time, your rabbit will let you know when he wants head petting. He will start approaching you, placing his paws in front of him and lowering his head.

Bonded rabbits assume this same position when they groom one another. Once he starts approaching you for head petting, you can be sure that trust is being established and a good bond has been created.

Petting your rabbit's tail or bottom area is different. It mimics what a predator would do in the wild. If a rabbit detects a predator, he will use quick evasion techniques to get away. For that reason, predators surprise rabbits by sneaking up and catching them from behind. Even though your pet rabbit is bred for domestic purposes, his natural instincts are still intact.

Avoid petting his hind area until he trusts you. Sometimes, even a good bond is not enough for a rabbit to let his guard down. Whatever the case with your pet, respecting his preferences and practicing patience is necessary.

Bonding your rabbit with other animals is an entirely different topic which is not addressed in this book. For information on bonding rabbits with other animals, visit *loveyourrabbit.com* or other online resources.

Jana Brock

Chapter Nine
Holding Your Rabbit

Lila: Did you hear that, Bandit?
Bandit: I didn't hear anything.
Lila: It sounds like an owl hooting outside the window.
Bandit: Don't worry, I will protect us.
Lila: Owls pick up rabbits with their claws and then fly away. They are incredibly frightening.
Bandit: Honestly, Lila. They are no match for my karate skills.
Lila: Do you really think you know karate well enough to scare off such a strong predator?
Bandit: I may not even need my karate. Honestly, look at me. An owl might take one look at me and decide it's not worth the risk.
Lila: Weighing in at two whole pounds…

Most rabbits do not like to be picked up, even by their owners. Your rabbit may stand on his hind legs and look directly at you or other family members. Humans are sometimes confused by this behavior.

When you see this behavior, rest assured your rabbit is not begging to be picked up or held. He is just trying to get a better view of what is going on above ground level.

Rabbits in the wild stand up, but they want nothing to do with being lifted from the ground. That is what happens when a predator captures them.

Fear of Being Lifted

Think about a large predator bird like a hawk or owl capturing a wild or domesticated rabbit. As the bird carries its meal away, the rabbit watches the ground get further from view. Picking up your rabbit and bringing him up to your height would, of course, give him a similar feeling.

Since a picked-up rabbit feels as though he is in great danger, he does anything he can to get free. This is a natural response and part of his base nature.

Fear of being lifted is not the only problem. People have lost their pet rabbits due to spinal and other fatal fractures because of improper handling or falls that result from unsafe carrying.

Since you must sometimes lift your rabbit (despite his fear), learn safe handling techniques. This will ensure he does not become injured in the process.

If your rabbit is not used to being handled, avoid abruptly picking him up. It is much better to sit on the floor and allow him to come to you. This stress-free method lets him know he is safe and that he can trust you in the future. In time, you can get him used to being held on your lap, picked up and safely carried.

Safety First

Some pet owners hold their rabbits in the air for selfie pictures. In that situation, one hand is used for the cell phone or camera and the other is needed to hold the rabbit. This means the rabbit's body is not properly secured, nor supported.

Depending upon his size and weight, such positions can cause a rabbit to be critically injured. With no proper support for the hind area, his weight pulls on his upper body which will stress his spine and other body parts.

Some pet owners carry their rabbit on their shoulders. This is irresponsible handling and very dangerous. While it might attract attention from onlookers, you can be sure a rabbit in that situation is searching for an opportunity to launch away.

Rabbits are ground animals. Their strongest instincts tell them they are safest with all paws on the floor. They will put themselves at risk of injury or even death to escape when they feel unstable or unsafe.

When you practice safe handling methods, your rabbit will get used to being picked up and even carried. It will also lessen his fear, reduce stress and ensure that there is no opportunity to harm himself trying to get back to the ground.

Pick Him Up

Finding the balance between making your pet rabbit comfortable and keeping him safe is easier than it might seem. Historically, rabbits were often mishandled. Today, we know better.

Never pick your rabbit up by the ears, scruff, tail or legs. Using those outdated methods of handling causes pain and injuries, even if the rabbit does not object vocally.

If you have a heavy or large rabbit, it is best to kneel to ground level and let him approach you. Pet him on the head to keep him calm. Slide one hand under his front legs and gently lift, leaving his back feet on the floor. Place your other hand on his hind end (bottom) area to support his weight, and then lift him up.

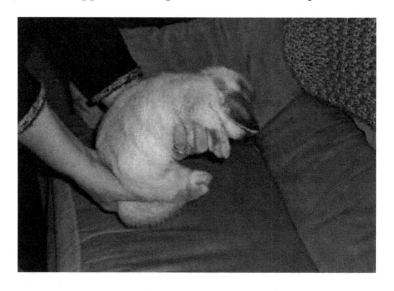

Make sure you maintain a safe and firm grip so that he cannot wiggle, twist, kick or launch himself into the air. Stand up after you have properly secured him. Of course, smaller breeds like Holland Lops (such as Lila, pictured above) are easier to handle.

Good Associations, Bad Associations

Pet rabbits quickly learn to associate being picked up with either a bad experience or a good one. You want your rabbit to associate human handling with safety and security.

You also want him to know that he's not going to be crated every time you come near him. Let's say that each time you pick up your pet rabbit you put him into a small container (pet carrier) where he is trapped. It doesn't take long before he associates being picked up with being trapped.

Another example of association is pet carriers and cars. Let's say your rabbit only sees his pet carrier when he goes somewhere. If you pick him up, place him into his carrier and then take him for a car ride, he will associate the carrier with scary car rides. Most rabbits are very stressed out when they must ride in vehicles.

You can use associations to your advantage. Sit on the ground with your rabbit. Pick him up and then put him back down. Let him play for a few minutes and then repeat that process a few more times. At the end of the practice session, give him a small rabbit-safe treat. This helps him associate being picked up with something he likes.

Likewise, it will be easier to get him into a pet carrier when he learns that *carrier* does not always mean *scary car ride*. Take the pet carrier into his space when you do your picking-up practice sessions. Set it on the floor near you and just leave the door open.

If he goes inside the carrier, don't shut the door. Just let him investigate. He will come out when he is ready. This will help him get used to the carrier without automatically associating it with riding in your vehicle.

Set Him Down

If you loosen your grip prior to setting your rabbit down, he will probably go into escape or launch mode. Remember, rabbits are genetically wired as prey animals, so escaping the grip of anything (or anyone) is instinctual.

Be mindful of his ability to launch himself into a nose-dive toward the floor. This could injure his delicate front legs, neck or spine. Keep your grip firm until he is at ground level.

If you are not already sitting, carefully lower yourself down so that you are not bending all the way over to ground level from a standing height. Such maneuvers are difficult and can be unsafe with a rabbit in-hand.

Set his hind legs down first and then his front legs. Once set free, your rabbit might thump the floor or hop away with his back feet kicking outward. This is quite common. It is just his way of expressing displeasure with a process he does not particularly like.

Football Carry

Learning to safely carry your rabbit is a must. There are excellent videos online from credible pet rabbit experts demonstrating this carrying method. It is advisable to review videos from responsible rabbit owners so that you can learn this skill.

When using the football carry method, pick up your rabbit and tuck him under your arm. His head should be between your elbow and side – much like you would carry a football. You should practice this while sitting on a chair so that if you accidentally mishandle him, he will not fall to the ground.

Using the football method, your rabbit's bottom/tail should be facing the direction you are walking. Keep a comfortable, but firm grip on him. Hiding his little head between your elbow/arm and your side keeps him calm. This method of carrying provides a dark retreat-like place for your rabbit's head and ensures his delicate spine is properly supported.

After you have him in the carrying position, place your other hand over his back for added support and stability. This way, he cannot wiggle out or get free. He also cannot see the ground or his moving environment. When done correctly, your rabbit should be quite calm and comfortable.

Chapter Ten
Crating Your Rabbit

Me: Hey, Bandit. Could you go into your enclosure so I can vacuum this room?

Bandit: I'm hiding in my tunnel.

Me: I can see you.

Bandit: What? Are you sure?

Me: Yes, I am sure. Your hind legs and feet are sticking out.

Bandit: They are? I thought this was a good hiding place.

Me: Not so much.

If you use a crate or large animal cage for your rabbit's primary space, he may want to retreat to it at times throughout the day. For this reason, cage or enclosure doors should remain open so he has free access.

Of course, there are times when you will need to intentionally crate your rabbit or place him in a pet carrier. This process will be greatly simplified by practicing proper bonding and handling methods as mentioned in the previous chapter.

Crates and Pet Carriers

When cleaning his outside-the-cage area, it is sometimes necessary for your rabbit to be locked in a crate or cage. He will also need to be in a pet carrier to be transported to a bunny sitter, veterinarian or other locations.

As always, avoid chasing your rabbit. If he evades you each time you approach him, he may feel as though he is in a predator/prey situation. This will not serve either of you well. It may take some time to turn things around, but it is never too late to practice better methods.

Crating or placing a rabbit into a carrier may take a few minutes, so allow yourself extra time. Rather than chasing, grabbing and then tossing him in, try a less stressful method.

Get a treat he likes, such as parsley, cilantro or a raisin. Rabbits learn to recognize words like "treat" which can be helpful. From ground level, wave the treat in front of his nose to coax him toward the crate or carrier. Toss it in so that he follows and allow him to eat it once inside.

After he enters, do not slam the door. Instead, slowly close it when you are sure he is clear of all moving parts. Coaxing a rabbit into any enclosure may take a few minutes and some patience on your part. It also helps to get him used to his carrier when he is not required to go in, as discussed prior.

If you do not have any luck using the treat method, use light-weight pet fencing. Gently enclose a space around the rabbit and the open crate or pet carrier. Slowly and carefully move the fencing closer and closer so that the animal has no choice but to go inside.

As with the other method, give him a treat once inside, even if he wasn't particularly cooperative.

You can gently shoo him inside once he is close to the carrier or crate opening. Never bump or hit him with the fencing (or any other object, for that matter). Also, never spray him with water or yell at him. Doing those things will only make him leery of you and fearful of the process you are trying to teach him.

Rabbits will generally respond favorably to basic training when their human owners are consistent, patient and kind.

Jana Brock

Chapter Eleven
Healthy Environments

Lila: You know why that bunny is in an enclosure?
Bandit: No. Why?
Lila: She got a time out.
Bandit: What's a time out?
Lila: It is something you should know about since you are always doing things you shouldn't.
Bandit: Like what?
Lila: For starters, stealing my food.
Bandit: I keep telling you it's not stealing. It's helping.
Lila: Fascinating how your brain works.
Bandit: It really is.

Rabbit housing can be a tense topic for those who care about the health and well-being of these animals. Providing an appropriate living space is very important, yet historic misunderstandings are still widely distributed today.

Rabbits must have plenty of space to exercise. Simply tossing them into a cage with pellets, water and hay would make any rabbit miserable (and sick). Since we hold our pet rabbits in captivity, we must accept the responsibility of meeting their basic needs. One of those needs is space to run and play.

Needs Will Vary

Small rabbits, such as dwarfs, require less space than average-size breeds (Lionheads, Rex breeds and Angoras, Mini Lops, et cetera). Giant rabbits will need an even larger area.

Adult rabbits, depending upon the breed, can weigh anywhere from 2.5 pounds to 25-plus pounds when they reach adulthood. When planning for living space and supplies, it is important to know how big your rabbit will get, on average, when he reaches adulthood.

Worth noting, terms can be confusing when researching rabbit breeds. Words such as "mini" can be used differently depending upon the information source. Two of my pet rabbits are Holland Lops. They will each weigh 2.5 to 3 pounds in adulthood.

My Mini Lops are larger than my Holland Lops. Adult Mini Lops average 6.5 to 8 pounds. Since Mini Lops are the larger breed, the words used to describe Holland Lops and Mini Lops do not really make sense. Words also vary from country to country. A dwarf breed in America might be called something different in Australia or Europe.

Conflicting verbiage aside, choosing the right primary house or enclosure requires careful thought about your pet's needs. You can choose from homemade pens or houses, pre-made houses, pet playpen materials, animal fencing, large crates, et cetera.

By informing yourself prior to getting a pet rabbit, you can save yourself from having to address problems later.

Enclosure Bars

A word of caution about the bars on cages, crates and pet fencing. They should be close enough together to make sure your rabbit's head cannot fit through any openings.

Your rabbit will likely try to force his head through any small space it can, especially fencing or cage bars. The head can then get stuck as he struggles to get free. This can result in a broken neck – a lesson you don't want to learn the hard way.

If the bars are big enough that the head fits through easily, the rabbit will naturally try to force his body through the bars, too. Again, there is great risk of getting stuck.

Because rabbits will do anything to get unstuck, they will violently thrash, which can cause fractures or internal injuries. For these reasons, any bars or holes in a pet enclosure should be smaller than the size of your rabbit's head.

Flooring

An important consideration is cage or enclosure flooring. Historically, wire mesh floors were used to house rabbits. They were mostly for human convenience. Meanwhile, the health and basic needs of rabbits were largely ignored.

Wire mesh should never be used for any rabbit enclosure flooring. Some rabbit owners say that thicker gauge wire is preferable. Still others say that solid flooring is the only appropriate surface for a rabbit's delicate paws.

One thing is certain. This topic can cause debate among rabbit owners who either support non-solid flooring or stand against it. Whatever your position, this topic warrants careful thought.

As with any published information, opinions form based on studies, reports and whatever might be popular at any given time. Since domesticated rabbits are still largely understudied, it is very important to understand the context of available information.

When researching this topic, consider a few common-sense questions. Were house rabbits used in *long-term* wire flooring studies? If so, how many? What breeds? How large were the rabbits? Were the rabbits studied housed outdoors? How many years were these rabbits observed on both types of floors?

Was each house rabbit involved in the study involved in health tracking? If so, over how many years? What was the process of measuring the difference in cleanliness between the two floor types? How many times per day were solid and non-solid floors cleaned and sanitized?

If you look closely at the actual studies used as the basis for non-solid flooring, much of the information used has been challenged. Some of the published information is not even based on house rabbits, but rather animals used for agricultural and other purposes.

Without getting into the finite details of each study, report or opinion, let's just quickly examine a few points used to support wire flooring and then examine some points of contrast.

Toenails

Those in support of wire or other non-solid flooring say that too-long toenails can cause the feet of a rabbit to sit incorrectly on solid floors. Rabbits in the wild, of course, have dirt beneath them which allows the toenails to sink in. In other words, the Earth has some "give" to it.

When on solid flooring, a rabbit's toenails cannot sink into soft ground, so too-long toenails might cause the rabbit's feet to sit in a position which might cause problems later. At least, that is the claim made by some who support wire floors.

It is true that too-long toenails can cause problems. They can push the toes and feet into a position that is not comfortable. The rabbit can eventually develop sore spots on the top of his toes and paws. This causes him to pick at the sore areas, which creates other problems.

The first thing that should be addressed here is responsible rabbit care. Pet rabbit owners must be willing to keep their animal's nails trimmed to an appropriate length. With proper toenail care at home, toenail problems should not occur.

As an aside, if you are not confident trimming your pet's nails, a rabbit-savvy veterinarian can teach you. Additionally, there are many excellent how-to videos on YouTube and other internet sites.

When in doubt, do some research. In this case, the visuals are very helpful. Depending upon your rabbit, nail trimming should be done every three to four weeks.

When considering wire floor information, it is also helpful to think about natural rabbit habitats in their entirety. Rabbits (and hares) populate much of Earth's land areas. They can be found in deserts, mountainous and rocky regions, coastlines, forests, suburban locations and even in extremely cold climates.

In all locations, they stand, run and jump - even on snow and ice. Ice, of course, is a very hard, unyielding surface. Clearly, there are many different types of natural ground surfaces that range from very soft to very hard.

That said, you can travel the world over and you will never find a place where nature provided rabbits with wire flooring.

Fragile Skin and Calluses

Some published information supporting wire floors suggests that rabbits have enough fur to protect their feet and if not, they will develop calluses. Keep in mind your pet rabbit does not have thick pads on the bottom of his paws like many other animals do.

Calluses sometimes naturally occur on the hocks of older rabbits. Otherwise, they are typically the body's forced response to harsh or painful pressure.

If wire flooring is the only option in a rabbit's living space, is he expected to form calluses on his body, too? After all, rabbits lay down quite frequently. The skin beneath their fur is thin and quite fragile.

Regardless the information that exists in support of wire floors, expecting a rabbit to develop calluses so that he can tolerate his environment seems unkind.

Happy Rabbit Tip

Consider purchasing rabbit-safe carpet remnants or rolls of indoor/outdoor carpeting to cover smooth surface or slick floors. Avoid using artificial turf or other harsh, plastic-like materials.

Creating a safe, long running path where your pet rabbit can safely exercise will help you meet one of his basic needs. It also protects your home's permanent flooring.

Since your rabbit has fur-covered paws, covering smooth or slick floor surfaces will also prevent him from sliding around. Watching a rabbit lose his footing on a slick surface might seem entertaining, but this can result in a broken spine, broken legs or other serious injuries.

Sanitation

Cleanliness is often used to justify wire flooring. Healthy rabbits eliminate waste often. Unless the potty spots are cleaned and sanitized almost constantly, the animal will have frequent contact with his own feces and urine.

In solid floor environments, a litter box is used. That means a rabbit's urine and feces are contained in one place. Rabbits do not live in their litter boxes. Conversely, many in a wire floor environment are forced to live on the same floor where they eliminate waste.

Some rabbit owners use a hose to clean wire flooring and might also sanitize it occasionally. However, water alone cannot eliminate the multitude of bacteria present in a rabbit's feces and urine.

When done properly, it should be easy and quick to train your rabbit to use a litter box. Litter boxes are easy to clean and sanitize because they have a smooth surface - much different than the never-ending intersections of a wire floor.

Risks of Injury

Wire flooring is surely more convenient for the owner. But what about the risks of injury?

Any opening in a wire floor that is large enough to pass rabbit feces through is also large enough for the rabbit's toe to get caught in. When that occurs, the animal struggles to free himself which can cause cuts and fractures.

Since rabbits are not complainers, these types of injuries often go unnoticed by humans and the animal suffers in silence. Wire floors can also cause sore hocks and a myriad of other potentially serious issues.

Though injuries can occur to rabbits regardless their living environment, the risks involved with wire floors are obvious and inherent. Those same risks do not exist with solid flooring when living spaces are properly prepared and maintained.

Chapter Twelve
Using A Litter Box

Bandit: Hey Lila, can you pass me some fresh hay?
Lila: Huma just refreshed the hay in both our litter boxes.
Bandit: I can't eat mine.
Lila: Why not?
Bandit: It's not clean.
Lila: She wouldn't put dirty hay in your litter box.
Bandit: She didn't. I wasn't paying attention and peed on it.
Lila: Of course you did...

Learning proper litter box training and maintenance is important. When they are set up and maintained properly, litter boxes are easy for the human and safe for the animal.

Most pet rabbits that live indoors are easily trained. If you live in an area where your bunny lives happily and comfortably outside, he can be trained as well.

Litter Box Maintenance

Pet rabbit owners sometimes make the mistake of prepping their rabbit's litter box just as they would do for their cat. Rabbits are not cats. Though they might occasionally dig in their boxes, most do not intentionally cover their urine and feces.

When using safe wood shavings or other litter, try putting a small amount into the bottom of the box. The litter should be a thick covering on the bottom – about two inches deep.

As your rabbit deposits urine and feces, take a handful of litter and cover those potty spots. Covering the used areas with a handful of fresh litter prevents your pet rabbit from stepping on his own potty when he uses it the next time. It also prevents the fumes of urine and feces from being air bound. Do your best to never allow a heavy layer of black feces to accumulate on the top.

If you are away from your rabbit during the day, establish a habit of going right to it when you return home so that you can quickly cover potty spots with fresh litter.

Consider using two litter boxes if your rabbit's primary space is an x-pen or similar type of enclosed area (anything other than a cage). When one box is messy, he can hop over and use the other.

Using litter types such as hard wood or other rabbit-safe wood shavings provides a nature-made material, though hay is an easy, popular choice. When maintained properly, nature-based litters will drastically reduce or eliminate odor.

Wood Shaving Litter

The information that has been distributed about wood shavings and rabbits is a topic that warrants careful examination. It is often taken out of context and distributed without solid review of the original study which has been used to justify it.

For this reason, some people are convinced that all wood shavings are unsafe. However, many experienced rabbit owners have used all types of wood shavings for decades with no associated problems. Still, it is wise to err on the side of caution.

Pine and cedar shavings naturally have phenols. These phenols account for the odor or strong smell that hits you in the nose when opening a new bag. Some studies suggest that those fumes can be linked to liver problems, cancers and possibly other health issues in small animals.

Pine and cedar shavings that have gone through a process to remove the odorous smell caused by phenols are considered safer. However, they are not always available. When they are, they might be more expensive.

When researching this topic, it is important not to make a sweeping determination that all soft woods are unsafe or all hard woods are safe. There are many factors associated with wood categorizations. It is a big topic which has not been comprehensively studied specifically in relation to domesticated rabbits.

Regardless conflicting opinions, rabbit owners often avoid untreated pine and cedar shavings. Fortunately, agricultural supply stores typically sell wood shavings made from aspen, fir, birch, et cetera. A wide variety can also be purchased online.

Other Litter Options

Among the most popular litter box options is to simply use newspaper and hay. This method is safe, easy to maintain, encourages more hay consumption. It is also one of the easiest and fastest ways to train rabbits to use a litter box.

To use the newspaper and hay method, line a clean litter box with newspaper and then stack a layer of hay on top. Since it is natural for rabbits to eat hay while going potty, this method provides a natural eating and elimination experience.

Instead of newspaper, you might line the box with an inch of wood shavings and then stack the hay on top. Either way, the point of lining the box is to absorb the rabbit's urine.

Hay is easy for rabbits to stand on. Since their waste falls through to the bottom of the litter box, paws stay cleaner. If you are away during work hours, the hay method is a great option.

Some rabbit owners add a small layer of hay in the evening before bedtime. Depending upon the size of your rabbit, you should clean the newspaper/hay (or wood shavings/hay) box every other day.

To clean, just dump the contents of the box and use white vinegar to wipe down the bottom and sides. White vinegar neutralizes urine and is much safer than bleach or other harsh chemicals. After cleaning just reline the box, add hay on top and it's ready to go.

Paper-based litters can also be used, although many rabbit owners do not like them and neither do the rabbits. This type of litter is a large type of pellet. Pellet litters can be more difficult to find locally and are typically expensive. Also, some rabbits like to eat it or chew on it.

Litters that contain dust, such as clumping cat litter, should never be used for rabbits. Also, use caution with plastic liners. Some rabbits are attracted to these liners and might chew them or, worse, eat small pieces. This could result in a blocked airway, intestinal blockage or other problems.

New rabbit owners often ask about using shredded newspaper, but it can be messy business. Loose paper quickly gets soaked with urine and feces. It then sticks to the litter pan where your rabbit is standing. It also sticks to your rabbit, which can cause urine scald.

Regardless the type of litter you choose, monitor your rabbit to make sure he is not eating anything in the box except hay. If one type of litter doesn't work after a week or two, switch types and try something different while monitoring closely.

Some new rabbit owners believe that rabbits need bedding such as wood shavings, shredded paper or hay on the floor of their primary living space. This is not necessary and, in fact, can inhibit litter box training.

Putting litter material in a rabbit's living space might also create unnecessary problems with sanitation since waste is often deposited beneath those materials where the owner cannot see it.

For bedding, consider providing old towels, packing blankets or other rabbit-safe cloth. These bedding options can be placed in the laundry so that your pet's living space is kept clean.

Even though house rabbits are bred for domestic purposes, they are still creatures of nature at their base. Some will reject manmade materials entirely and only use what nature would provide for them if they lived in the wild.

Jana Brock

Chapter Thirteen
Primary Living Space

Lila: Huma built us a new house. It's so big!

Bandit: It is a nice home, but the pet fencing is too tall. How will we jump out when the door is closed?

Lila: We aren't supposed to do that.

Bandit: Jumping is my job.

Lila: You don't have a job.

Bandit: I have a job. I do bunstruction projects. Just yesterday I tore up a phone book.

Lila: That is different than trying to escape.

Bandit: I didn't say I wanted to escape.

Lila: Then why do you care about jumping over the fence walls?

Bandit: It's just what I do, Lila. Don't overthink it.

There are many good options for indoor rabbit housing. If you use a premade cage or animal crate, make sure it has ample space for your rabbit and a rabbit-safe floor (never wire mesh!). Floors should be easy to clean and sanitize.

Because typical made-for-rabbit cages are often too small to be a primary rabbit residence, consider expanding the space. There are many ways to accomplish this task and ensure your rabbit's environment is safe and spacious.

Expand Primary Space

Rabbits are no different than other active animals. They get frustrated being confined to a cage all day. Over caging can also cause health problems over time. In the wild, rabbits have access to unlimited space. Likewise, domesticated rabbits need plenty of room to exercise every day and, if possible, during night hours. A spacious environment helps keep rabbits happy and healthy.

Even if you use a cage as primary space, you can easily add a play area for your rabbit using pet fencing and leaving the cage door open. Be sure to secure the cage door when it is open so the rabbit doesn't shut himself out or get caught in a swinging door.

You can add a yard, of sorts, outside his cage-door opening. Pet fencing that is 34-inches tall works well for most house bunnies that are of average size. Doors in pet fencing can also be left open, especially if the room is already rabbit-proofed. If you do not have a rabbit proofed room, adding some enclosed space outside the cage is the best option.

A word of caution about pet fencing or other primary living space. Make sure your rabbit cannot climb out (yes – some rabbits try to climb non-solid walls!). This is rare, but it has happened. Observing your rabbit will let you know if he is a skilled climber.

When adding space to your rabbit's primary living area, it is also important to consider floor protection. Particularly true of young unaltered rabbits, carpeting and other flooring can easily be ruined by marking, digging or chewing. It can also suffer damage during the litter box training stage. These problems are easily avoided by covering permanent flooring.

Rolls of indoor/outdoor carpet can be purchased at a low cost at most supply stores or you can order it online. You can also use old carpeting, inexpensive or second-hand area rugs or carpet remnants (low pile only). Most rabbits will dig at, and even eat, high-pile carpeting which is why low-pile carpeting strips or rugs are the safer option.

Rabbit-safe carpeting allows for no-slip running and jumping. Of course, like any floor covering, carpeting needs to be kept clean.

Some rabbit owners use plastic overlays or slick, smooth linoleum to protect their permanent floors. This may be easier to clean, but it is not easy for rabbits to navigate. Since a rabbit's paws are covered with fur, slippery surfaces cause instability – much like a human walking on a sheet of ice.

If you were forced to walk on a surface where you feel unstable, you would eventually get used to it. However, you would always be at risk for falling and sustaining a serious injury. The same is true for rabbits. Getting a good grip on slippery surfaces is impossible when your feet (paws) are furry.

Yoga matting or other such materials are not good options because many rabbits find them chewy and irresistible. If your rabbit eats pieces of plastic or soft matting, he could develop a serious digestive blockage which would put his life at risk.

Pet Fencing Enclosures

Fencing comes in all shapes, colors and sizes. Some brands are easier to work with and can be assembled/disassembled easily. As discussed prior, avoid pet fencing that has bars or spaces large enough for the head or body to fit into or through.

Rabbit-safe fencing or pet playpen panels simplify the process of increasing or decreasing your rabbit's space. Moving these types of enclosures or fence panels to other rooms is quick and easy. It can also be used for supervised outdoor play time.

Some pet playpens are equipped with a pet door. This enclosure material can be found on Amazon and other sites for $40-$60 (or more). The price depends upon the type, brand and how many panels you wish to purchase.

Lila and Bandit made a list of things they need from the store. They don't like to ride in the car, so they asked me to do their shopping.

Lila wants curtains, a blanket and her own hay feeder. When I asked what was wrong with the hay feeder they have now, she said that Bandit dumps the hay onto the floor and then pees on it. She doesn't want to hurt his feelings, but his hay-peeing habit is very hard for her.

Bandit had one thing on the list. He wants a raisin.

Chapter Fourteen
Rabbit Proofing - Cords & Cables

Bandit: I found a cord yesterday.

Lila: Did you chew on it?

Bandit: I couldn't because it was covered.

Lila: That's good.

Bandit: What do you mean, that's good? Cords are chewy.

Lila: Huma covers them so that we don't get hurt.

Bandit: I wouldn't get hurt.

Lila: The electricity would burn your mouth. You wouldn't be able to eat or drink.

Bandit: I'm tough. I could handle it.

Lila: You are ridiculous.

This chapter addresses an important step in rabbit-proofing your home. Whether your pet has free roam or is confined to a smaller space, cord protection is a must.

Old Methods of Cord Protection

A quick scan of the internet provides several ideas for keeping your rabbit away from electrical cords. Some say to cover your cords with soap, bitter sprays or other such products. The idea is that by applying a topical substance, rabbits will be repelled.

There are several problems with that method of cord protection. For starters, it rarely works long-term. Also, applying substances to your cords is kind of like washing your child's mouth out with soap as a punishment for using a swear word.

Covering cords with soaps, liquids or sprays is not a compassionate thing to do. It could also make a rabbit very sick if he is persistent. Since more safe and effective options exist, it is best not to resort to those tactics.

Out of Reach Cords

When researching, you might see information telling you that keeping cords higher than your rabbit's reach is enough. This would work for high outlets, but most houses have plug-ins close to the floor. Also, rabbits are curious in nature and will stretch or jump to investigate things which are not good for them.

Some rabbit owners suggest placing cords under carpeting, which is unsafe because it creates a fire hazard. The same hazard exists when hiding cords beneath furniture that is on the floor, meaning there is no space between the bottom of the furniture and the floor itself.

You might have success hiding cords behind furniture. Just keep in mind that rabbits are burrowing animals, so they fit into surprisingly small spaces. Many a pet owner has discovered that their rabbit squeezed himself beneath a couch or chair where he wasn't supposed to fit.

As an aside, when your rabbit has access to the underside of couches, chairs or beds, he might chew holes in the lining (which is likely made of fiberglass). He will then crawl up into the furniture's springs. If he doesn't chew a hole, he will work at a corner of the lining until it loosens and creates a space to crawl into. It is quite common for rabbit owners to overlook these problems because humans do not typically examine the undersides of their furniture.

Defacing the underside of furniture results from a rabbit's natural instincts. After all, beneath your furniture is a dark, retreat-like space, which is attractive. Even so, it is important to think about the potential consequences of allowing your rabbit this type of access.

Sitting on a couch or living room chair when your rabbit is hiding in the springs is a real problem. It could squish him, fracture his spine, break legs or cause other significant injuries. He could also keep investigating until he finds the cords you thought were out of reach since they were behind the furniture.

If your rabbit does find a cord you thought was out of reach, he will make short work of chewing it in half. Getting a hold of the wrong cord will cause serious burns to the mouth, jaw, face and tongue. Those injuries might be invisible to you, but they will harm him. Worst case scenario, it could result in critical burns or fatal electrocution.

Three-Step Cord Protection

The risk of cord chewing is greatly reduced or eliminated by using a combination of safe techniques. Keep cords out of reach, absolutely, but also cover them. By adding cord coverings, you protect your electronics and your rabbit.

Cord wrap can be found at many appliance stores, on Amazon and in other market outlets. It is inexpensive – generally under $10 for 20 to 30 feet. Cord wrap is available in varying sizes so that all cords within your rabbit's reach can be quickly and easily covered.

Since many rabbits also chew cord protectors/cable wrap, we suggest added protection by making a fabric covering which you will use as an outer layer. Double-protecting cords is often overlooked by rabbit owners, yet it is highly effective.

Making a fabric cord covering is easy and inexpensive. It just requires a small piece of scrap fabric (which most people can find around their home), a needle and some thread.

Cut an oblong piece of fabric. Fold it in two and bring the sides together. This forms a fabric tube, of sorts.

Sew it along the cut sides, leaving the top and bottom open so it can slide over the cord. The longer, the better. Unplug the cord and slide the fabric tube over it. If you are concerned about appearance, you might purchase a piece of fabric to match your home's décor.

The fabric cord cover will extend from the plug up to the cord itself and prevent the animal from having easy access. After investigating a few times, rabbits usually decide it's too much trouble and will leave double-covered cords alone.

In the image above, the three-step process of cord protection has been used. 1) The cord is out of reach (pulled upward rather than draping down and resting on the floor); 2) Flexible cable wrap was applied to the cord itself; and 3) A homemade satin-type fabric tube was used to cover the plastic cord wrap.

Using smooth or slick, satin-type fabric for the cord covering works well because it slides downward and covers the plug where it goes into the wall. Rabbits that can reach it will have a hard time getting a grip and quickly lose interest.

Chapter Fifteen
Rabbit-Proofing - Furniture, Walls & Deco

Lila: Bandit, can you move your bunstruction project somewhere else? I need more space.
Bandit: I'm busy right now. Trying to fix this carpet.
Lila: Huma didn't like it last time you fixed the carpet.
Bandit: That's why I'm fixing it better.
Lila: How are you going to do that?
Bandit: I'm making a bigger hole.
Lila: Unbelievable.

Protecting Furniture and Walls

Furniture legs are often made of wood. For that reason, they are very attractive to your pet rabbit. Most rabbits will chew on walls, baseboards and molding – whatever is at floor level and within reach. As you can imagine, it does not take much to deface or destroy an otherwise beautiful home.

To reiterate, it is not appropriate to discipline your pet rabbit for doing what comes natural. That said, some rabbit owners have had some success training their pet rabbits away from areas of temptation. Still, this type of training is often not reliable long-term because curiosity in rabbits is a persistent trait.

Even if it appears to work initially, relying on training is risky. Supervision is still necessary. If you get distracted, he could do some extensive damage in a short amount of time.

Give your rabbit a variety of safe toys. Toys will keep him busy and entertained. They also lessen the chance of him chewing your home to the ground.

Even with toys, it is wise to place wood barriers between the animal and all areas of concern. The positive side of placing barriers everywhere is that you don't have to worry as much. Additionally, the rabbit will chew more wood which is helpful in keeping teeth ground down.

The downside to using so many barriers is it can change the appearance of an otherwise nice space, even when they are tastefully placed. Painting or staining barrier wood is risky because those substances are toxic to rabbits.

It is not realistic to permanently cover every couch, chair, table, dresser and bed with pieces of natural wood. If you are going to do that, you may as well make your entire house a rabbit cage and go live outside with the squirrels.

Cardboard can also be used as a bunny barrier. Just keep in mind that some rabbits have a propensity to ingest regular cardboard which can lead to intestinal blockages. Those situations rarely end well.

If used, cardboard should be thick and not easily torn. Heavy gauge cardboard the thickness of postal or shipping tubes are better. The thicker the cardboard, the more likely your rabbit will chew it rather than eat it.

If you choose to use wood barriers around your home, research pre-made barriers. Another option (much less expensive) is to build your own. Building your own allows you to customize the appearance and size of the barriers.

Of course, you could do what so many other rabbit owners do and just use pet fencing to section off a bunny's accessible space. If you use fencing, you can allow him access to certain areas at certain times because it is easy to move.

Whatever method you choose, your rabbit should always have access to his food, water and litter box.

Fake Plants and Other Décor

Many rabbits will chew on or even eat fake plants. Since they chew so quickly, it only takes a few moments to cause harm. Eating plastic or other such materials might cause a serious or fatal intestinal blockage.

Once a year, Christmas trees go up. Cords from lights are exposed, ornaments hang down and presents are at ground level. That means extra precautions must be taken.

Regardless the season, it is best to move fake plants and other harmful-for-rabbit décor out of reach so that your bunny never has access. During the holidays, gate off your Christmas tree with pet fencing when your bunny is roaming free. Conversely, you can keep the tree in a room not accessible to your rabbit.

Assume your pet is interested even if you do not see him going near these items. It just takes a moment of diverted attention for him to find trouble.

Jana Brock

Chapter Sixteen
Relaxation

Lila: Do you have to chew so loud? I'm trying to get some rest.
Bandit: Geeze, Miss Hormonal. Relax.
Lila: You did NOT just tell me to relax.
Bandit: Okay. How about chill out?
Lila: Try again.
Bandit: Settle down?
Lila: Nope.
Bandit: This is very difficult.

By nature, prey animals are very guarded. They have adapted to watching and listening for predators. Staying somewhat ready to evade predators is a rabbit characteristic, even in the safety of your home.

Sleeping Rabbits

Is your rabbit asleep or awake? Since rabbits often sleep with their eyes open, sometimes the only way to tell is to watch the nose. Your pet rabbit's nose will wiggle almost constantly when he is awake. When he is sleeping, his nose stops and rests.

Some new rabbit owners believe their pet never sleeps. This is a misconception. Rabbits often sleep in a guarded position – head upright and eyes wide open. If you must interrupt a sleeping rabbit, do so very gently to minimize the risk of startling. Otherwise, it is best to come back later.

Rabbits were once thought to be nocturnal animals. Today, they are categorized as crepuscular. This means they are most active near the hours of dusk and dawn.

Being crepuscular does not mean they are not active other times. Rabbits can be quite sporadic with what times of day they are awake or asleep, though most are believed to rest more during daylight hours. Of course, they are observed more during the day because that is when humans are typically awake.

Sleeping rabbits can become very active with legs kicking, eyes moving rapidly, teeth grinding, ears raising and head moving. It looks much like the rapid eye movement (REM) stage of sleep for humans.

Though no one can prove whether rabbits have dreams, upon close observation it appears they have stages of sleep. This is not unlike what other mammals experience.

Purring

Happy rabbits have their own way of purring. When you pet your rabbit's head or face, he may show his contentment by lightly grinding his teeth. From the front, it almost looks as though he is talking very softly.

Light tooth grinding is different than what you see when a rabbit is in pain. If your rabbit is grinding his teeth loudly when you are not petting him or he grinds them harder than normal, something may be wrong.

Observe him closely for additional signs of injury or illness. If teeth grinding continues even when he is not being petted, it is best to contact your veterinarian and have him examined.

Jana Brock

Chapter Seventeen
Rabbit-Safe Treats

Bandit: Huma, we would like an apple.

Me: You can't have an apple.

Bandit: We had a little taste once.

Me: Yes, but that was a very small bite for a very special occasion.

Bandit: Why can't we have them more often?

Me: They cause diarrhea, diabetes and teeth problems. Plus, they are much too high in sugar. Rabbits in the wild rarely come across fruit. Apples are not one of your regular foods.

Bandit: If you give us an apple, we promise not to eat too much.

Me: I'm sorry, Bandit. I just cannot do that. You can have some salad in a while.

Bandit: With raisins?

Me: No raisins.

Bandit: Sheesh…

Giving your rabbit the occasional treat is okay if the food provided is not harmful to him or overfed. Allowing him to eat something that is not good for him might make him happy at first. However, by the time you realize your mistake, he might be very ill.

Most manufactured foods should not be fed to your pet rabbit, even as an occasional treat. Some made-for-rabbit snacks contain flour, dairy products and other things these animals should never eat. Rabbit treats might even be labeled as healthy when the truth is, they are not.

Yogurt snacks that contain dairy should never be given to rabbits since they are strictly herbivores. Other manmade treats, such as most rabbit biscuits, likely contain chemicals and preservatives. It is wise to avoid them.

When choosing rabbit-safe treats, using nature as a guide is good practice. If you use any fruit as a treat, make sure it is no more than a small piece (coin-sized). Allowing your rabbit to consume half an apple or a bowl full of fruit will likely cause diarrhea or other problems.

Your rabbit may not show immediate effects of feeding him the wrong treats or too much of one type. However, poor dietary practices that are not immediately obvious can cause health issues in the long term.

Chapter Eighteen
Veterinary Care

Lila: I need to see a veterinarian.
Bandit: What is a veterinarian?
Lila: A doctor for animals.
Bandit: What for?
Lila: I just need a checkup.
Bandit: How do you know?
Lila: We girls just know these things.
Bandit: I don't need a rabbit doctor. I can take care of myself.
Lila: What if you get sick or injured?
Bandit: Honestly, I'm so tough that I don't worry about it.
Lila: I see. Kind of like a superhero.
Bandit: Exactly.

Having a rabbit-savvy veterinarian can make a huge difference in the life of your pet. Rabbit owners must be aware that some vets treat rabbits even if they have absolutely no rabbit specialty training or consistent hands-on experience. For this reason, it is important to call around and find one who is qualified.

Rabbit-Savvy Veterinarians

Rabbits need to see a qualified veterinarian. They need physical exams and need to have their teeth checked. They will likely need surgeries or even emergency care at some point. Of utmost importance is having the right vet spay or neuter your rabbit if that has not already been done.

A common mistake made by new rabbit owners is to assume that all exotic animal veterinarians are rabbit experts. This is not true. Some exotic animal vets are rabbit experts, but it is not because they have been trained in the broad category of exotic pets. Not all exotic pet veterinarians are experienced with rabbits.

There is a lot to consider when providing medical care to rabbits. For example, they can die if given certain antibiotics or pain killers even when other animals tolerate them fine. Informed rabbit owners and rabbit-savvy vets are aware of these issues.

Other factors should be considered when choosing a veterinarian. Some vaccinate rabbits even when it is unnecessary; some administer common flea/tick products which cause problems; some still send rabbits home with absolutely no pain medication after spay/neuter (or other) surgeries; and some have no idea the types of foods a rabbit should eat and/or avoid entirely.

If a veterinarian does not understand at least the basics of at-home care and handling, he or she will likely not know the problems that arise when a rabbit eats something it shouldn't. That is important because so many rabbit problems arise from improper diet and digestive problems.

When fed improperly, a rabbit can get diarrhea, have constipation or a full-on intestinal blockage. Those problems lead to a rapid health decline and can quickly cause death.

Being genetically wired as prey animals, rabbits are not complainers. They do whatever they can to hide symptoms of pain and illness. Rabbit-savvy veterinarians are aware of this reality and understand what to look for when they see one that needs rapid medical intervention.

It is also important to realize that veterinarians often do not have house rabbits at home so they are not familiar with hands-on, day-to-day care and practices (other than what they might read or "hear" from others).

If your vet does happen to have his or her own house rabbits, it is a real bonus for you. Otherwise, do not expect them to be experts on behavior, housing options, best toys, home protection ideas, bonding, et cetera.

Ask Questions

It is a good idea to call around before settling on a rabbit-savvy veterinarian. Ask questions. One place might say that rabbits are easy and any exotic pet veterinarian can treat them, even if they don't see them regularly. If that is the case, keep searching until you find a vet who sees rabbits on a regular basis.

In many areas, rabbit-savvy veterinarians can be difficult to or even impossible to find. Do your best to avoid choosing one just because it is near your home. It is important to research and inform yourself of what experienced rabbit owners already know. Online research is most often free and is worth the investment of time.

Once you have equipped yourself with enough rabbit-related knowledge, make some calls and ask some questions of the veterinary clinic you are considering. It is most helpful to at least ask the following questions.

How many rabbits are seen each week? What kind of rabbit diet does the veterinary recommend? Does he/she routinely vaccinate pet rabbits that live in the house? How many spay/neuter surgeries are performed on rabbits each week? Does the vet send a supply of pain medication home after surgery?

Finding a veterinarian who sees house rabbits regularly and is current with rabbit-related information will give you peace of mind. It will also ensure your pet has the best care possible.

Jana Brock

Chapter Nineteen
Altering: Spay/Neuter

Lila: I heard the humans talking. Today you are getting neutered.
Bandit: What does neuter mean?
Lila: I'm not sure, but you will have to ride in the car.
Bandit: Will you come with me? Cars are terrifying!
Lila: I don't like to ride in the car, either.
Bandit: What if you see a clown while I'm gone? I won't be here to protect you.
Lila: You are afraid of clowns, remember?
Bandit: I've grown up. I am a lot braver than I was back then.
Lila: It was just a few days ago.
Bandit: Seems longer.

Most pet rabbit owners are not professional breeders. That being the case, there are good reasons to spay or neuter pet rabbits as soon as they are old enough. The world, in general, has an overpopulation of wild and domesticated rabbits.

Even the most seasoned pet rabbit owners know that things can go wrong when rabbits undergo surgery. It is true that there are risks. However, statistics show that the benefits of altering rabbits far exceed those risks.

Reasons to Alter Your Rabbit

There are many reasons to alter your pet. For starters, you don't want to add to the overpopulation problem. Alteration surgery is especially important for rabbit owners that have a male and female pair.

Rabbits have a reputation of being frequent breeders – and for good reason. They can reproduce at an alarming rate. There are several reasons why this is true.

Females do not ovulate on a monthly schedule. They ovulate when they mate. Also, rabbit pregnancies last an average of 30 days, depending upon the breed.

Most rabbit litters can average four to five kits, though larger breeds sometimes produce twelve or more. Litter size also varies depending upon the breed. Most females, after delivering a litter of kits, can get pregnant again in the next day or two.

If your rabbit does get pregnant, there are things you must do to prepare. Online information can help. In addition to caring for your pregnant rabbit before and after delivery, you will need to responsibly rehome the kits after eight weeks of age.

Many rabbit kits die because of improper care or handling. If your rabbit kits do live, finding a home where they will each be properly cared for can be difficult. Of course, if you have only one rabbit or if your pair is the same sex, there is no risk of pregnancy but there is still good reason to spay or neuter.

Surging hormones bother most rabbits. They also cause an increase in undesirable behaviors. A week or two after your rabbit is altered, you should notice a significant reduction in digging, scratching, marking territory, anxiety and aggression. The decline of these activities is a sign that your rabbit is no longer being tortured by constant hormone surges.

Marking territory with urine or feces is natural for unaltered rabbits, though it can still occur after surgery if other animals are in the area. Bonding animals helps with territory marking because they learn that their space is shared rather than owned.

For females, getting spayed is also a safeguard against ovarian cancer and other serious health problems. Altered rabbits generally live longer, happier lives and are more calm and friendly.

Since rabbits do not vomit, they should never fast prior to surgery. General anesthesia is typically used for alterations of both bucks and does.

Spay

To accomplish alteration, female rabbits are spayed. While sedated, the uterus is removed and the incision site is then closed using stitches.

Most rabbit-savvy veterinarians will use dissolvable stitches which will be hidden beneath the skin. This prevents the rabbit from chewing on them post-surgery.

Neuter

Males are neutered. This is often referred to as castration or desexing. To stop future sperm production, the testicles are removed.

Veterinarians who are current on rabbit science will likely use a pre-scrotal method of neutering rather than scrotal neutering. Scrotal neutering (the old way of altering males) removes the testicles through the scrotum which causes unnecessary pain and swelling.

Separate males from fertile females during the healing period. Not only is this safer for the post-surgery rabbit, but sperm can still be present after the procedure. Neutered males are less aggressive. Barring any problems, they also have a better chance of living a longer and happier life.

Post-Surgery Care

Information on post-surgery care varies and can be somewhat conflicting. It is helpful to research this topic since not all sources (and veterinarians) agree on what to do when you get your rabbit home.

All altered rabbits, male and female, should come home with at least four to five days of rabbit-safe pain medication, such as Metacam. You should receive instructions on how to safely administer it.

It is critical to ask your veterinary clinic about post-surgery pain management prior to scheduling any surgery. If the clinic does not believe that rabbits need post-surgery pain medication, find a more compassionate provider.

Taking care of your pet's pain helps alleviate symptoms so that eating and drinking resumes on time. That said, it is normal for rabbits to refuse food after surgery.

Typically, post-surgery rabbits resume eating and drinking late that night or the very next day. To ensure your rabbit has the best chance of getting back on his regular eating and drinking schedule, administer pain medication on time and as instructed.

After returning home, make sure there is fresh hay and pellets (if used). You can also leave greens such as fresh parsley, green leaf lettuce, dandelion leaves, or cilantro. Even a small amount of food will keep his digestive system moving.

To keep tasty green treats fresh, snip the ends of greens and put them in a shallow bowl with water. The fresher it stays, the better. If it wilts, remove it and replace.

Force feeding right after surgery is typically unnecessary (and could be risky) unless you are experienced and can do so without causing him stress. This is no time for your rabbit to be wiggling, twisting or thrashing. His stitches could break loose or he might experience internal bleeding.

Some information suggests that you should give your rabbit whatever he wants to eat after surgery, such as apples, pineapple or other fresh fruits. However, extreme caution should be used.

The surgery itself is somewhat of a shock to the rabbit's system. Radical diet changes or too much fruit could cause the digestive system to get further out of balance. This could cause diarrhea. If that occurs, you will have a dangerous situation which creates further problems or even put his life at risk.

It is helpful to provide fresh water in a shallow bowl, even if your rabbit usually drinks from a water bottle. Choose a bowl that will not tip over easily. Bowls provide a more natural drinking experience and can also prevent additional pain that might otherwise be caused by reaching for a water bottle spout.

No other animals should have access to your post-surgery rabbit's food or water. If they are allowed access, you really cannot know for sure what, or how much, the rabbit is consuming. Containing him in a small area for a few days helps. It also ensures he does not move around more than he should which helps with healing.

To put your mind at ease, you might spend a few minutes reading online information at credit rabbit information websites. Reading post-surgery information on rabbit society or pet rabbit organization websites will give you a good idea about what to expect following surgery.

If you feel your rabbit is outside the scope of what is considered normal or other problems arise, you should call your veterinarian.

Other Considerations

A clean litter box and living space is always important, but extra effort should be given when a rabbit returns home from surgery. You need to be able to monitor your rabbit's post-surgery waste elimination (poops). A clean litter box and living space helps immensely.

Rabbits are shaved prior to surgery so there is a bald place at the incision site. If your rabbit's fur does not immediately grow back, there is usually no cause for concern. It is not uncommon for several months or even a year to pass before surgery site fur returns to normal.

Bonded Rabbits

There are some considerations for bonded rabbits when one of them gets altered. Some information sources say not to separate rabbits after surgeries because they will not bother one another.

It helps to take both rabbits to the veterinary before the surgery. However, when you return to pick up your freshly altered rabbit, it is best to leave the other one at home.

While some bonded rabbits may appear to do okay together after one of them has had surgery, it is risky. Humans cannot supervise rabbit interactions 24 hours a day because they must sleep and do other things. For that reason, it is not logical to say that bonded rabbits should never be separated for any reason.

A freshly-altered rabbit could be critically injured if in tight quarters with another animal, regardless the prior bond that existed. Also, post-surgery rabbits need to rest. It is logical to expect they feel tired, strange and may experience some pain even with medication.

If you do not separate bonded rabbits when one has had surgery, you might see the post-surgery rabbit being chased, harassed and forced to keep moving as he tries to protect his incision from his partner.

A post-surgery rabbit will not be acting normally, especially the first few days back home. His partner knows something is amiss and just wants to investigate. A post-surgery rabbit does not need that kind of attention.

At the very least, the post-surgery rabbit is run ragged trying to get some quiet space where he can just rest. His partner trying to investigate might not occur while you are supervising but could be happening when you are not there.

Unnecessary movement puts your post-surgery rabbit at risk for problems. It can also enhance pain and cause immense stress. In this situation, bonded animals can fight and display other behaviors not normal for them. If left in the same space post-surgery, they can start behaving as though they were never bonded at all.

When separating bonded rabbits after surgery, good practice is to give them constant access to one another (so their noses touch) through a pet fence or playpen panel during the entire healing process. That way, they can still interact but are not in the same space.

After a period of healing time (one to two weeks, depending on whether you deem it safe), slowly reintroduce them while closely supervising. This will minimize risks of injury and ensure that things quickly get back to normal.

Chapter Twenty
Food Pellets

Lila: Huma, can Bandit and I have some more pellets?
Me: It looks like you ate your morning pellets. You can have some more tonight.
Bandit: But pellets are delicious.
Me: I imagine they are but if you keep eating pellets, you won't eat your hay. Without enough hay, you would both get very sick.
Lila: That makes sense.
Bandit: Okay, but when we go outside again I'm going to find a pellet tree.
Me: It will be right next to the raisin bush.

When given the choice, most rabbits will forego hay and just eat pellets. Pellets, regardless the quality, are manmade foods. Rabbits do not eat them in the wild.

Years ago, pellets were originally manufactured to force rapid weight gain in rabbits used for meat and/or lab testing. Those pellets were not sufficient for long-term health or proper nutrition.

Though most people do feed their pet rabbit a small amount of pellets, some do not. If you do not use them, it is important to research what foods to give your rabbit to ensure he has a balanced, healthy diet. Information sources, such as credible rabbit-related websites and books, will help you understand daily nutrition needs and which pellets are best.

Choose Wisely

Over time, higher quality pellets have been developed so that pet owners have better options. Whatever healthy diet you choose for your pet rabbit, keep in mind that not all pellets are created equal.

Cheap, low-quality pellets contain fillers that can cause health problems. Some now have genetically modified foods added which animals should not consume.

When choosing pellets, the following is recommended as a baseline: 18% fiber; 12-14% protein for adults and about 16-17% for rabbits less than 5-6 months old; calcium – no more than 1%; fat 2.5-5% and the appropriate Vitamins - A, D and E. Of course, this information can vary depending upon your information source.

Pellets such as Oxbow, Ecotrition and other brands are considered high quality and can be purchased online, at most pet stores and rabbit-savvy veterinary clinics. Pellets should have a young rabbit option as well as those made specifically for adults. A quick internet search for will help you make a good decision on which branch to choose.

Adult rabbits should eat no more than one-quarter cup of pellets per day for every five pounds of body weight. So, a seven-pound adult rabbit should have no more than just over one-quarter cup. You can feed half the pellets in the morning and half at night, or you can feed the entire amount once per day.

Pellets have a pull date. Some experts say you should not use pellets that are two to three months from date they were manufactured.

If using pellets that are older, carefully inspect them to make sure there is no foul odor, no mold, moisture or discoloration. If there is any sign that they did not stay fresh, throw them out and replace them with new product.

Happy Rabbit Tip

Bonded rabbits sometimes steal food from each other. If you feed them together, make sure they are both getting their correct portion, especially leafy greens and pellets (if used).

If they quarrel at meal time, you might separate them while they eat. That way, neither will become obese and they will both get the nutrition they need.

Chapter Twenty-One
Rabbits And Vegetables

Lila: Why do you dump our salad onto the floor?
Bandit: Bowls are for little kits. We are getting older.
Lila: We are still young rabbits. What's the rush?
Bandit: Older rabbits get more treats.
Lila: Huma already gives us treats.
Bandit: I know, but those are vegetables. I want big-rabbit treats, like raisins.
Lila: How will eating from the floor help?
Bandit: It makes us look more mature.
Lila: Are you joking?
Bandit: Nope. It will help us get more treats.
Lila: Well, it doesn't make sense to me.
Bandit: Just let me do the thinking.
Lila: I don't even know how to respond to that.

The information here is provided as a general guideline. You may need to adjust basic information depending upon your rabbit. Some have illnesses or special needs which may be different than what is considered normal. If this is the case with your pet rabbit, you should seek expert advice and adjust your rabbit's diet accordingly.

Align with Nature

Rabbits have a very sensitive digestive system. Kits typically nurse five to six weeks after they are born. During this time, they will eat the scraps of vegetables and hay that their mother eats in the nest. This helps adjust the flora in their gut which helps to prepare them for a regular diet.

Good eating habits start when rabbits are very young. This includes proper hay consumption, vegetable consumptions and high-quality pellets (if used).

Varying information can be found on feeding pet rabbits, so it is important to pay close attention to the source. When in doubt, it is good practice to stay in alignment with nature and what it intended for rabbits. It is also helpful to remember that rabbits are strict herbivores but that does not mean that all plants are safe for consumption.

One example is corn which is, of course, nature-based. While most experts say that rabbits should never be fed corn or corn products, some information suggests that the husks are safe and can even be beneficial because of the fiber.

Who knows the long-term effects of corn husks in a rabbit's diet? Historically, they may have been fine for consumption. However, we must consider present day realities. Things have changed since GMOs (genetically modified organisms) made their way into our food supply.

Studies on animals fed GMO products provide enough information that we can assume they will compromise animal health when regularly consumed. Had nature intended for animals to eat human modified foods, GMOs would have always existed. That is not the case. In addition to humans intentionally altering what nature provided, consider what rabbits do in the wild.

When thinking about safe foods, the height of your rabbit is important. If he were living in the wild, he would forage for ground foods or those which he can easily reach. Corn (and hence, the husks) are not normally within reach.

As stated previously, not all natural plants are safe to consume. Nature has a plethora of plants which may be toxic, or even poisonous, to rabbits – domesticated or wild.

Fortunately, there is a wide variety of vegetables and plants known to be safe when fed in proper quantities. Sticking with tried and true feeding practices will help with long-term health and assures the digestive system remains in proper balance.

Feeding Young Rabbits

Baby rabbits should not be separated from their mother until they are at least eight weeks old. Prior to taking a new rabbit home, regardless his age, find out what he has been eating.

Keep your new bunny on the same diet he has been on for a week or longer. Rehoming causes enough stress. The last thing you want to do is cause him to become ill by abruptly changing his diet.

As rabbits age, they should be introduced to fresh, clean, organic greens. Most tolerate slow diet changes beginning at about 12 weeks old (3 months). Parsley, cilantro, dandelion leaves, romaine lettuce (in small amounts), safe plants/stalks and tree leaves and baby kale (if tolerated) can all be slowly introduced into your rabbit's diet.

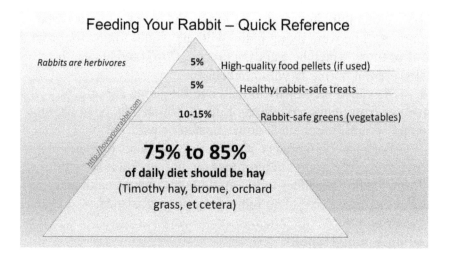

Feeding Your Rabbit – Quick Reference

Rabbits are herbivores

5% High-quality food pellets (if used)

5% Healthy, rabbit-safe treats

10-15% Rabbit-safe greens (vegetables)

75% to 85%
of daily diet should be hay
(Timothy hay, brome, orchard grass, et cetera)

http://loveyourrabbit.com

The information in this chart is not all-inclusive. It aligns closely with basic feeding guidelines of domesticated rabbits, though information sources and opinions can vary. The 5% treat category includes fresh fruit, which can be fed occasionally in very small amounts.

Feeding can vary depending upon age, health and other factors. If your pet has needs which are outside the basic guidelines for feeding, you should consult with a rabbit-savvy veterinarian or obtain information published by other domesticated rabbit experts.

Cruciferous Vegetables (Brassicas)

Some vegetables, such as kale, are often overfed to domesticated rabbits. This is because they can be found on safe-to-eat food lists. That said, it is not wise to assume that a food that is deemed safe for your rabbit means you should provide it on a regular basis.

Brassicas is a genus of plants belonging to the mustard family. Brassicas are better known as *cruciferous vegetables*. Kale, broccoli, brussel sprouts, mustard greens, cabbages and cauliflower are examples of cruciferous vegetables.

According to a study done by a professor at the UW Department of Horticulture, cruciferous vegetables, or brassicas, should be fed sparingly. There are a few reasons why this is true - one being a compound called glucosinolate, which is produced by brassicas.

In the wild, this glucosinolate compound discourages some animals and insects from eating or overeating it. If your pet rabbit eats it on a regular basis, microbes in the gut are disrupted, which then leads to an imbalance in gut flora. This disruption is caused by too few beneficial bacteria.

The overgrowth of bad bacteria allows the overgrowth of yeast and/or parasites. Some information suggests that these foods, when fed consistently, can also cause the thyroid to malfunction. Toxicity can build up in the rabbit's system and one problem leads to another. Soon, the animal's health is in a downward spiral that is difficult to identify or correct.

Since there are so many rabbit-safe vegetables and leaves that have no questionable side effects or health risks, many pet owners avoid cruciferous vegetables entirely or use them only as an occasional treat.

This does not mean you must never feed your rabbit kale or other cruciferous vegetables. This information is provided to show that misunderstandings can easily occur as a result of only looking at topical information or taking the advice of others without proper investigation.

Slow Changes

Since food tolerance and amounts can vary from rabbit to rabbit, it is important to introduce new foods and increase amounts very slowly. Your rabbit's digestive system needs time to properly adjust the gut flora when fed unfamiliar foods.

Adding several new foods too quickly can cause everything to fall out of balance. This can result in soft or runny stools, diarrhea, bloat, gas and other stomach upset.

It might also cause the overproduction of cecotropes. Cecotropes are clumps of smaller, shiny, black, odorous feces. While rabbits should never consume their normal waste, they do eat their cecotropes. This is necessary for them to get the nutrients they require for good health.

Any one of these problems can start a series of cascading events which quickly worsen if they are not promptly addressed.

The slow introduction method applies to all foods, including vegetables/greens. Try a small piece of romaine or red or green leaf lettuce (never iceberg!). Give your pet rabbit a small piece at first. If everything is okay, give him the same vegetable in the same amount the next day. And the next. Watch your rabbit's feces to make sure everything stays normal.

If no problems arise, you can add another rabbit-safe green such as dandelion leaves. His green diet then should consist of a very small piece of dandelion leaf and half a leaf of rabbit-safe lettuce. Repeat the process over the next few days while, again, closely watching his feces for any changes. If everything is okay, keep him on those two greens for up to a week before adding anything else.

A good measure of how much greens a rabbit should eat once he is used to them is no more than three-quarters of a cup or one cup per day for every 2-3 pounds of body weight. If your rabbit weighs six pounds at six months old, you can work up to feeding him more greens. Rabbit expert information regarding consumption of greens varies depending upon the source.

You can adjust the amount of greens per your rabbit's tolerance. Be very careful not to overfeed any vegetable, regardless the information that exists about its safety.

Rabbits can also eat some fresh grasses if they have not been sprayed or treated with chemicals. If you feed your rabbit a safe grass, it is best to let him forage it rather than cut it first.

If you do cut the grass and then feed it, do so immediately. Grass begins to rot once it is cut. Like any other food, rabbit-safe grasses should be introduced slowly to ensure proper tolerance and digestion.

Try feeding half of daily vegetables or greens in the morning and the other half at night. This helps ensure your rabbit's system adjusts properly and he doesn't get too many at once. If at any time his feces (poop) gets soft or other problems arise, discontinue the problem vegetable and feed more hay until his feces normalize.

Once the rabbit's droppings are normal again, you can start the vegetable/green introduction process over again. Reduce the amount of greens and keep close track of anything your rabbit does not tolerate. This will ensure you do not feed him a problem vegetable again in the future.

Establish a feeding routine and schedule. If your pet rabbit does develop persistent diarrhea, constipation, severe gas, ongoing digestive upset or refuses to eat at all, contact a rabbit-savvy veterinarian immediately.

Jana Brock

Chapter Twenty-Two
Sweets And Treats

Bandit: Huma, my salad bowl is empty.
Me: Yes, I see that.
Bandit: Aren't you going to fill it back up?
Me: You and Lila already had your morning greens.
Lila: I didn't get to eat all of mine.
Me: Why not, Lila?
Lila: Bandit ate his and then ate mine before I could finish.
Me: Why did you do that, Bandit?
Bandit: It looked like she needed help.
Lila: I don't need your help.
Bandit: It's okay, Lila. I got you.
Lila: Seriously…

Anything Sweet

Rabbits like sweet tastes and will also eat salty snacks. Even though he will eat them, your rabbit should never be fed cookies, candy, crackers, popcorn, et cetera. Manmade and chemical foods which are not meant for rabbits can cause problems in the digestive system and affect overall health.

Fruits are sweet so your rabbit will probably like the taste. Even so, there are several good reasons not to feed your rabbit too much fruit. A rabbit in the wild would not likely climb a tree to pick an apple or get a banana.

On the topic of rabbits and fruit, there is little variance of information. It only takes one experience caring for an animal with severe digestive upset or diarrhea to have a complete understanding of how dangerous too much fruit can be.

Fruit is high in sugar which can contribute to the onset of diabetes. When providing it as a treat, consider giving your rabbit a very small amount – a coin-sized piece of apple or banana. Or, you might give him a raisin, blueberry or small strawberry.

Contrary to children's fables, a steady diet of carrots is also not good for rabbits. Like fruit, carrots should only be used as treats. Provide a coin-size slice or occasionally add carrot peelings (or shavings) to your rabbit's greens.

Indoor Plants

Rabbits will chew on just about anything, including indoor plants. While your rabbit might view them as a tasty treat, ingestion could cause serious harm or even be fatal. It is important to keep your rabbit away from all indoor plants.

Your rabbit should also be prevented from having access to fake plants and other home décor. During the holidays, restrict access to your Christmas tree, regardless whether fake or cut.

Happy Rabbit Tip

Your pet rabbit is happiest when he is kept on a simple, nature-based (herbivorous) diet. Feeding him anything that his gastrointestinal tract is not equipped to deal with can cause an imbalance in his gut flora which leads to a myriad of health problems.

Jana Brock

Chapter Twenty-Three
The Importance Of Hay

Lila: You were digging in the hay. What were you looking for?
Bandit: I think Huma dropped a raisin in here somewhere. Help me look.
Lila: You are smelling the banana bread she made.
Bandit: Oooh, that sounds yummy. Maybe she'll give us some.
Lila: Rabbits don't eat bread. Besides, you are too little.
Bandit: I am not too little! Huma gave me a piece of carrot in my greens just this morning.
Lila: No, she gave ME some carrot and you took it out of my mouth.
Bandit: I try to be as helpful as possible.
Lila: Again, I do not need your help.
Bandit: Pretty sure you do.

In the wild, rabbits have unlimited access to fresh grass, dried grass, leaves, bark and other foods. Since nature is their garden, wild rabbits can maintain a balanced diet. When we bring them indoors, they rely on us to provide them with what they need.

A rabbit's daily diet should consist of 75%-85% fibrous, natural, chemical and pesticide-free hay and/or other course fiber. This means that your rabbit should always have unlimited access.

The amount of hay your rabbit should eat every day should equal the size of his body. Hay and course fiber is extremely important. It keeps the digestive system strong and is necessary for good health and longevity.

Types of Hay

Rabbits need a primary diet of Timothy, oat, brome, orchard grass or a combination of meadow and other rabbit-safe hays.

Alfalfa can be mixed with other hay when rabbits are very young. As the rabbit approaches young adulthood, it should be tapered off and taken out of the main diet.

Since alfalfa is a legume hay, it is rich in protein and calcium. In adulthood, absorption of too much calcium can cause kidney stones, urinary tract and other health problems.

Young rabbits tolerate alfalfa hay but it does not have the proper balance of nutrition for adults. Timothy, brome, orchard grass and other adult-safe hays have the proper balance of fiber, protein, calcium and vitamins to support nutrition needs of adult rabbits.

Your young rabbit needs to develop a taste for the hay he will be eating long-term. To accomplish this, mix his alfalfa with Timothy and other hays while he is still growing. Transitioning alfalfa out of the diet of a young rabbit will be more difficult if he has never eaten anything else. Of course, you can also use this transition method for an older rabbit that was not fed properly prior to you acquiring him.

Eliminating alfalfa from your rabbit's diet should occur slowly. As with other foods, harsh changes can cause problems. As your rabbit gets older, start decreasing the amount of alfalfa while increasing Timothy or other rabbit-safe hay.

Some veterinarians might suggest that young rabbits eat alfalfa hay until they are a year old. Conversely, experts with day-to-day, hands-on experience raising rabbits say that it should be phased out of the diet at about six months old.

As with many topics, conflicting information exists. Most rabbits that do not have alfalfa hay beyond six months old seem to thrive without it.

Digestion

The most important reason for proper hay consumption is a rabbit's digestive system. Timothy and other such hays have long fibers necessary to maintain digestive strength and health. If a rabbit does not have proper fiber, food will not digest correctly and his system can stop moving.

A rabbit that does not have enough course fiber in his diet can quickly succumb to Gastrointestinal Stasis (GI Stasis). GI Stasis is when the digestive system slows down and then stops moving.

This painful condition is commonly known as *the silent killer*. It can develop rapidly and has taken the life of countless rabbits within days of onset. GI Stasis can also be caused by intestinal blockages when a rabbit consumes something he should not eat.

While some medications and other factors can also lead to GI Stasis, it is most often avoided by proper feeding and care. A best practice of rabbit owners is to form a daily habit of checking feces (poops). In fact, this is a must!

If waste is not being eliminated normally (poops are decreasing in number and size, or are nonexistent), a veterinary appointment should be made. Time is of the essence.

Recovery from GI Stasis is possible, though once a rabbit experiences it the owner must be even more careful with diet and overall care. Rabbits that have had GI Stasis are more susceptible to it happening again.

When GI Stasis is not immediately addressed (or if treatment is not successful), the rabbit's exit to life could be immensely painful and traumatic. Pet rabbit owners who are present at the time of death are also traumatized because of the "screams" that occur prior to the animal's last breath.

Maintenance of Teeth

Rabbits have 28 teeth in the front and back of the mouth which grow constantly throughout life. They can grow 10 to 12 cm per year. Depending upon breeding and other factors, a rabbit's teeth can be a very complex and expensive problem.

Chewing is something your pet rabbit enjoys, but it is not the only reason he does it. If the rabbit does not have access to the course fiber he needs, his teeth will grow long and he will not be able to eat. Of course, that begins a series of cascading events that quickly spiral downward.

Course, fibrous hay helps immensely. In addition to unlimited access to hay, make sure you provide safe and clean tree branches, small pine cones, bark, hard wood blocks and other rabbit-safe chewable items.

Pet rabbits typically like to chew on cardboard items such as paper towel or toilet paper rolls. While some rabbits do okay with those items, some do not.

As mentioned prior, a good alternative is to use a heavier gauge item such as thick shipping tubes. They can be cut in half or into smaller pieces using a utility knife or jigsaw. Heavy cardboard is good for chewing but difficult to tear apart.

A rabbit will sometimes ingest cardboard or paper if he is not eating enough hay or getting enough other course fiber in his diet. Cardboard and paper products are not natural foods for rabbits. A little "too much" can cause severe blockages in the digestive system which, of course, can quickly cause GI Stasis.

When a blockage occurs, motility drugs and other procedures may or may not be effective in resolving the problem. If that is the case, the blockage can result in a harsh end to life. If your pet rabbit has a habit of eating carboard or paper, it is not a good idea to give him access to those items.

If you do provide cardboard or paper products, they should be free of color, glue and tape. If you give your rabbit phone books or newspapers, make sure the ink is not toxic. Soy-based ink is safer than petroleum-based inks.

Fresh Hay, Clean Hay

Rabbits are natural foragers. They want to dig and search for food, so they will often dig in their hay if it is on the ground. They will also use it for a potty place. Keeping hay clean and fresh is a daily chore.

It is best to have hay feeders secured to a wall at mouth-level. Some secure a hay feeder within comfortable reach of their litter box. This ensures they can nibble while going potty.

If you do not have a place to secure a hay feeder to the litter box or near enough to it, you can put hay directly into your rabbit's litter box either up against one side or across the top. In fact, hay in the litter box is considered a best practice. Of course, this is a moot point if you already use hay as litter.

While eating hay from the litter box, your rabbit may dig and forage through it to find desirable, clean strands. This is perfectly normal and no cause for concern.

All hay feeders should be checked and refreshed daily. Once every few days, totally dump the hay feeder so that dust from the hay will not accumulate on the bottom.

Happy Rabbit Tip

Rabbits are part of nature's Leporidae family (lagomorph). They are foragers. Even though your rabbit is not in the wild, his desire to forage is intact. One way to provide a natural experience is to allow him to forage indoors.

Place a towel down on the floor and put hay on top of it. Rather than feeding pellets from a dish, place them under the hay. Your rabbit will have fun foraging through the hay in search of his pellets.

Chapter Twenty-Four
Picky Eaters

Bandit: Huma, are you taking a picture of our feet?
Me: Yes, Bandit. Your feet are cute.
Bandit: Okay, but don't let anyone see it. My feet are kind of dirty.
Me: No one will mind.
Bandit: I don't want to get a dirty-feet reputation.
Me: Is that a rabbit thing?
Bandit: Of course it is.
Lila: It is NOT a rabbit thing...

Some rabbits are hay snobs, meaning they are overly picky or might only eat alfalfa. There could be several reasons for picky hay eaters. However, it often results from overfeeding pellets or treats and failing to encourage proper hay consumption.

It is important not to give up if your rabbit is refusing to eat hay. Your commitment to finding something that works could literally save his life. It cannot be overstated that a lack of course fiber in the diet can cause serious digestive and teeth problems.

Establish a Feeding Schedule

For this discussion, think of food pellets as candy since most rabbits love them. You would not give candy to your kids around the clock or before every meal. Getting them to eat healthy foods with such a poor diet would be almost impossible.

A 7-pound (adult) rabbit should have no more than about 1/3 cup of high-quality pellets in a 24-hour period. You can offer pellets in the morning and rabbit-safe greens at night. Or, you can provide half of the rabbit's daily greens and half of their allotted pellets in the morning, and the other half (of greens and pellets) at night.

Rabbit kits can have more high-quality pellets while they are gaining weight. Though rabbit owners, breeders and veterinarians somewhat disagree on this topic, providing unlimited pellets to any rabbit beyond five or six months old warrants some careful thought.

If you choose to provide unlimited pellets to your young rabbit, it is important to closely monitor him so that he is eating hay and greens. Some rabbits will ignore hay and greens when food pellets are always an option.

Most young adult and adult rabbits thrive when they are kept on a feeding schedule. This is because hay is the only food option available when it is not mealtime (mealtime, meaning consumption of pellets and greens).

That said, sometimes a feeding schedule is not enough to convince a rabbit to eat enough hay or encourage hay consumption after or during illness. In those cases, an extra "nudge" is sometimes necessary.

Sweeten the Hay

One of the best tricks to encourage more hay consumption is to sweeten it up. This works well if a rabbit has been ill, experienced GI Stasis or is just plain picky.

Rabbits love sweet tastes. This can be used to your advantage. Try breaking open a raisin or dried cranberry so that the softer inside flesh is exposed. Rub it down the length of several hay strands so they are slightly coated with the smell and taste.

Hand-feed your rabbit the sweetened hay strands so that you know they are being consumed. This process, of course, requires patience and time but is well worth the effort.

Be careful not to overdo it by leaving small pieces of the dried fruit on the hay. If you do, the rabbit will just pick the fruit pieces off (or lick it off the hay strand) rather than eating the hay itself.

Avoid the temptation of providing hay that has pieces of dried fruit in it when purchased. The reason for this is that most rabbits will forage through the hay to find the dried fruit. Over time, rabbits will just eat the fruit and leave the hay. Overconsuming dried fruit could cause serious digestive harm. This defeats the purpose of teaching good hay-eating habits.

The sweeten-the-hay trick also works well using banana, apple slices, the insides of blueberries, pineapple or other rabbit-safe fruits. Since rabbits should not have much fruit or sweet treats, sweetening hay should not be done long-term.

Over a few days (up to a week at most), start decreasing the amount of sweetness you add to the hay strands. For example, provide four hay strands that have the fruit added, and six that do not. Then, add fruit to two hay strands and provide eight that are plain. Add less and less until all hay is plain.

Hay Cubes

Hay cubes are about one-square inch and are typically available in timothy hay and alfalfa. These little cubes can be provided as treats. However, they can also be used when your rabbit refuses to eat regular hay.

Obviously, hay cubes are not found in nature. For that reason, it makes sense that they should not be part of the main diet of rabbits. They are certainly not an apt replacement for regular, long-strand hay.

Since sick or picky rabbits are more inclined to chew on these condensed cubes, they are good to use when regular hay is completely rejected (or if the sweeten-the-hay trick did not work). Hay cubes are better than your rabbit eating no hay at all.

Compressed Hay Bales

Buying small hay bales which are compacted or compressed can help your rabbit eat more hay. He will most likely enjoy pulling apart the bale because it mimics a natural foraging experience. Compressed hay bales can be found online or ordered through many pet and agricultural supply stores.

Hay at Potty Time

This information was provided in a prior chapter, but is worth repeating here.

Rabbits like to nibble on hay while using the litter box. Hay can be stacked up against one side of the box to ensure good access or it can be used as primary litter. Both are best practices that help encourage hay consumption.

Remember, another great option is to make a hay feeder that is within reach of a rabbit's litter box. Hay should be at about chin-level to your rabbit so that he can comfortable reach it when it is potty time.

Emergency Care – Don't Wait!

If your rabbit refuses to eat, has abnormal feces (or worse, diarrhea), stops eliminating waste all together or is having other such problems, you should call your veterinarian.

Chapter Twenty-Five
Rabbit Emergency Care Pack

Lila is so excited. She passed all her finals and will soon graduate from the AMFR (Academy of Modeling for Rabbits). When I asked her what she plans to do after graduation, she said, "I am thinking about studying abroad."

Since a rabbit's health can decline rapidly, owners need to keep some emergency care items together in what is called an emergency care pack. Emergency care packs can be large or small depending upon individual needs.

Your emergency care pack does not need to be anything fancy. In fact, you can assemble one at home. Having what you need on hand and knowing how to use those items can make a huge difference if your rabbit gets ill and cannot be immediately seen by a veterinarian.

Basic Emergency Supplies

Ideally, an emergency care pack should contain the following items: rectal thermometer; plain Neosporin (original); Simethicone (for gas/tummy upset); feeding syringes (2 tsp or 10 ml capacity – size of syringe will vary depending upon the breed/size of your pet); several large towels; gauze bandaging; sports wrap; saline solution and Critical Care for rabbits (can be stored in freezer to ensure it stays fresh). It is also helpful to keep a quick reference sheet with information on emergency care for rabbits.

Additional supplies that might be necessary can generally be found around your home, such as toenail clippers, mineral oil, heating pad, blunt-tipped scissors, hydrogen peroxide, extra towels, non-chemical (no dyes, scent, etc), cotton swabs and other wound care supplies.

Finally, include a card with your veterinarian's name, address and phone number. In an emergency that you cannot (or should not) handle on your own, veterinary information is easy to locate.

Chapter Twenty-Six
Syringe Feeding

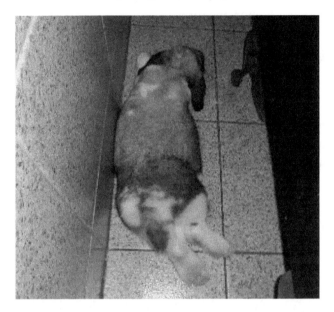

Me: Are you okay, Jo? You look a little sad.

Jo: I miss my humans.

Me: I know, but we will have some fun while you are here. I promise.

Jo: Where did they go?

Me: They went snowboarding. They will be back in a few days. Would you like some dandelion leaves?

Jo: No, I don't much feel like eating.

Me: I'm sorry, Jo. I know it's difficult. But, you know, it really is important that you keep eating and drinking while they are gone. If you don't, you will get sick. Being sick is no fun for rabbits.

Jo: I know. I got sick once and it was horrible.

Me: I'll get you some food and then you can go play with Lila and Bandit.

Jo: Okay.

If your rabbit becomes sick or injured and refuses to eat or drink, call your veterinarian immediately. When requesting an emergency appointment, most vet clinics have the option of dropping your rabbit off so that he can be seen at some point during the day when the doctor has time.

Dropping your rabbit off is a good option if you are comfortable leaving him and waiting for a phone call. Most animals will wait in a contained area (cage) until the veterinarian has time to squeeze in the exam.

Some rabbit owners are not comfortable leaving their pet until an appointment is available. If you choose to keep your rabbit with you until you can get a scheduled appointment, you will need to start syringe feeding so that his gut keeps moving properly.

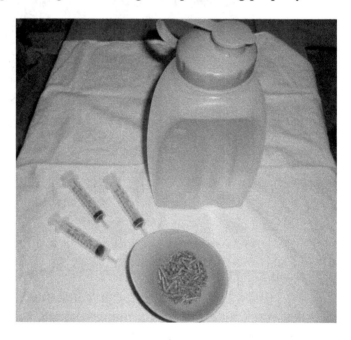

Syringe Feeding

Rabbits often refuse food when they are sick or in pain. They may also refuse water. We already know that a rabbit's health can decline quickly once eating and drinking stops. This can quickly lead to Gastrointestinal Stasis (GI Stasis). For this reason, syringe feeding is a necessary skill for all pet rabbit owners.

Feeding syringes can be purchased at veterinary clinics, pet and agricultural supply stores and other locations. They are typically less expensive when purchased online. Don't wait for an emergency to purchase one. Always keep several on hand.

In addition to syringes, emergency care food (such as *Critical Care* for small animals or a similar product) is a wise investment. Emergency care foods stored in the freezer will preserve freshness.

If you do not have prepackaged emergency care food, you can dissolve food pellets in warm water for several minutes. If the mixture is not the right consistency to easily go through a feeding syringe, add more water and stir until it is correct.

Non-sugar baby foods can also be used for syringe feeding. Choose rabbit-safe vegetables. Some rabbit owners also use pureed fruits but care must be taken since fruit can cause diarrhea.

You can make your own pureed emergency food by placing green, leafy vegetables into your blender. Add water, if needed, to ensure the puree will flow smoothly through a feeding syringe.

Pureed vegetables is a green drink, of sorts, for your rabbit. Adding high-quality pellets to the vegetable puree adds essential fiber.

Be as careful with vegetables as you would with fruits since too much can cause soft stools or even diarrhea. It is best to adhere to proper percentages for daily vegetable feeding, even when syringe feeding is necessary. Pellets and water (without vegetables added) can be used for subsequent feedings.

It is important to learn how to syringe-feed your rabbit correctly. If you do not, you could force liquids or food into his lungs which could kill him.

Your veterinarian or his/her staff can teach you how to safely syringe-feed your rabbit. If this is not possible, there are good videos on YouTube and other sites. Learn from a credible source that teaches non-stressful feeding techniques.

Some rabbits will allow you to syringe-feed without restraint. If not, you will need to safely wrap them in a towel. Feeding using a towel-wrap method is easier with two people. If you are syringe feeding your rabbit without help, fill the syringe and place it within your reach before wrapping him.

You can wrap and feed your pet on a counter top or table only if there is no risk of him jumping down or falling. Jumping or falling could cause fractures, other significant injuries and even death. Failing to consider the safety of your pet will only cause more problems for him and for you.

The safest practice is to place a large towel on the floor and put the rabbit on half of it. His head should be sticking out one end facing forward with you behind him. Fold the towel over the rabbit's body and bottom, enclosing him. Use your arms to safely hold it down so that he cannot twist, kick or wiggle free.

Once you have your rabbit enclosed in the towel, place your elbows on either side of the rabbit holding him firmly while leaning over him. Some rabbit owners call this a bunny burrito. It is a method which safely restrains your rabbit's legs close enough that he is firmly secured.

You should never wrap your rabbit in a towel, turn him on his back and then force feed him. All paws should be down whenever you are syringe feeding or administering oral medication.

Slowly Feed Small Amounts

Place the syringe into his mouth from the side where he has no teeth. Do not put the syringe between his front teeth straight through the middle of his mouth and then release a large amount of food.

Give him a very small amount at a time – about 2 to 3 ml for a rabbit that weights 5 to 7 pounds. Decrease dose for smaller rabbits and increase for larger breeds, as appropriate. Remove the syringe and allow time for him to either chew or swallow the mixture.

Let him rest before you give him more and repeat this process until you have fed him the appropriate amount for one feeding. Proper syringe feeding requires patience and takes time.

For an average size rabbit, experts say you should feed about 10 ml of the mixture every few hours until he starts eating on his own again or until he can get veterinary care. You can also syringe-feed your rabbit the water he needs so that dehydration does not occur.

If your rabbit refuses to chew or swallow what you have fed him (it just drains out of his mouth), or if he is basically not responsive to the process at all, you should take him in for emergency veterinary care without delay.

Jana Brock

Chapter Twenty-Seven
Toys And Retreats

Lila: Huma, what is this tube thing?
Me: It's a rabbit tunnel. You can run through it.
Lila: So, it's a toy for me and Bandit?
Me: Yes.
Lila: We have a lot of toys.
Me: I don't want you to get bored.
Lila: Bandit loves new toys, but he would rather have more treats.
Me: I'm sure he would.

Keeping a rabbit occupied is important. They are playful creatures that need a lot of toys. Also, it is important to provide one or more rabbit retreats (hiding places).

Rabbit Retreats

Thick cardboard boxes provide a great retreat for rabbits. Cut a hole for a door and a window. You can also buy or build cardboard castles and other structures.

Whichever type of playhouse you buy or make, your pet rabbit will stay busy using his teeth to customize it. He will be eager to give retreats that personal touch.

Retreats are part of a basic rabbit need. Instinctually, they go underground for protection in the wild.

Some people believe that rabbits in nature live above ground. This is a common mistake. If you come across a rabbit-like nest that is above ground, it likely belongs to a hare. While hares and rabbits are mammals that both belong to the Leporidae family, they are not the same species.

Hares live in above-ground nests. They are larger than rabbits and have bigger ears. Though the coat colors can be quite similar, many hares have black tips on their fur.

A hare is not as social an animal as the rabbit. Their kits are born with hair and can hop within hours of their birth. There is a myriad of other differences, but they are of little importance here because most people do not have hares as house pets.

Conversely, wild rabbits live in underground burrows. A warren is an underground system, or network, of burrows connected by tunnels. This information is important when bringing a rabbit indoors. Retreating to dark, tunnel-like places is instinctual and provides a place to escape, relax and feel at ease.

Tunnels

Every house rabbit needs at least one tunnel. These are typically made of untreated or unstained wicker or tree branches. Some are also made of wire which is covered with cloth.

Grass tunnels are also an option, but most of those unravel quickly. Cloth-covered cat tunnels are a favorite with rabbits. They are longer and provide an area your pet will love to run through. All types can be found online starting at around $8-$10, though costs will vary depending on product source and shipping costs.

Play tunnels are also available in plastic, though care should be taken to protect your rabbit, as some use them for chew toys. The danger, of course, is that your pet could ingest the plastic which would cause damage to a rabbit's internal system. Plastic tunnels can easily be covered with a homemade cloth sheath to ensure your animal is safe.

Oblong items such as large cardboard shipping tubes can be used, as can long cardboard boxes. If you use these items for your rabbits, be mindful of the size. Some tubes are a size that barely allows the rabbit to fit into it. If that is the case, find something larger.

Since rabbits are attracted to small spaces and will squeeze themselves in, you must ensure there is a way back out. In the wild, rabbits have dirt, grass or other earthy materials to grab onto. This makes it easy for them to move forward or backward so they do not get stuck.

Carboard is a smooth, slick surface that provides no traction for a rabbit's fur-covered paws. Your pet might get partway into a small tube and stay there, unable to move. Whatever rabbit-safe item you use, make sure there is at least an inch of free space on all sides of the animal when it is in a hunched position (sitting on his hind legs).

Safe Toys

Saving your pet rabbit from boredom is a must. Rabbits are very curious animals. They need to chew, explore and have plenty of mental stimulation.

Toys should be free of toxins, paints, tape, glue and other harmful materials. Most rabbits will play with and cuddle stuffed animals. Make sure the eyes and other parts are either removed or secure enough that they cannot be chewed off. Ingesting plastic parts, such as the eyes, could be harmful.

Natural grass mats and grass tunnels are excellent rabbit toys because they are safe to chew and ingest. Rabbits will also play with small hard wood blocks and clean branches. Branches can be cut from rabbit-safe trees such as apple and other fruits.

Natural wood toys keep your pet occupied and encourage chewing. This helps your pet's teeth stay ground down to a healthy, proper length. Your pet rabbit should always have plenty of safe-to-chew materials.

Other toys that rabbits like include durable plastic stack-up cups; sturdy tent balls; phone books (printed with soy-based ink); stainless steel stacking cups or measure cups (without handles); wooden spoons and spatulas (unstained only).

Chapter Twenty-Eight
Rabbits And Water

Lila: Huma, I want to stay outside longer.
Me: I know, Lila. But it is getting dark.
Lila: I can see fine in the dark.
Me: Yes, you have excellent vision. But there are other problems.
Lila: Like what?
Me: Well, for starters, I can't see as well as you can. What if a big owl comes and tries to take you? Owls are predators. They come out at night.
Lila: (looking up to the sky) Owls are scary.
Me: Yes, and they love small rabbits like you and Bandit. Also, it is not good for you to get wet. It is already starting to rain.
Lila: I don't like to get wet.
Me: I don't blame you.
Lila: We should go in the house now.
Me: That sounds good.

Not long ago, there was a video circulating on the internet. A rabbit owner had placed his pet rabbit into a swimming pool and videotaped it as it struggled to keep swimming. Of course, the rabbit owner found this entertaining, which was apparent listening to the laughter on the recording.

As the rabbit swam around, it kept looking up at the side of the pool. Any responsible rabbit owner could clearly see that the animal was desperately searching for a way to climb out. Disheartening, to say the least.

It is hard to believe that people still subject their animals to what many people view as unethical practices, especially for nothing more than human entertainment. Rabbits being placed in swimming pools outrage experienced rabbit owners who understand that the animal is terrified in that situation. Also, the chemicals in a pool or hot tub can burn a rabbit's tender, thin skin.

Rabbits are not built for long periods of strenuous exercise. They evade predators by sprinting short distances, and then they must stop. Swimming is immensely exhausting. You should never place your rabbit in such a body of water for any reason.

Bathing

Some rabbit owners have been misinformed about bathing rabbits. In the absence of illness or other harsh circumstance, bathing your rabbit is totally unnecessary and can also be unsafe.

Rabbits are prodigious groomers, much like cats are fastidious cleaners. This means that under normal circumstances, rabbits constantly groom themselves and stay quite clean. They do not have skin or body odors like many other house pets.

Unless your rabbit is ill and has had soft stools or diarrhea, he does not need, nor want, washing assistance. Cleaning a soiled bottom is the exception.

Sometimes, an illness or injury may prevent a rabbit from grooming himself or reaching his bottom. If that occurs, humans should only wash the area that needs to be cleaned. This must be done very gently and with no chemicals or harsh soaps.

In addition to your rabbit keeping himself clean, bathing him is traumatic. He would likely respond with immense anxiety and fear. He can also jump and twist trying to get out of the water, which can injure his spine.

Other bath-related problems can also occur, such as shock due to a drastic change in body temperature. Also, a rabbit's fur is not easily dried – even with a low-heat hair dryer (which, if you are not very careful, will burn his tender, thin skin).

In nature, rabbits do not jump into pools of water or streams or rivers for pleasure. They also do not immerse themselves in water to bathe. Barring extraordinary circumstances, humans should adhere to nature's process and let rabbits clean themselves.

Happy Rabbit Tip

Pet owners sometimes dress their rabbits in tight-fitting shirts (or other clothes) and then take pictures. While entertaining for humans, the process of dressing a rabbit can be a traumatic experience. It can also be dangerous when the animal wiggles and tries to get away since rabbit legs and spines are fragile.

Rather than putting a shirt or other fitted clothing on your rabbit, drape it across his body instead. You can then take a picture and quickly remove the item. That way, there is no risk of harm and the animal is not traumatized.

Chapter Twenty-Nine
Outdoor Time

Thank you for letting me come outside to play. Amen.

Rabbits are nature's children. The species originated in the wild, though breeders have mixed genes and created different types for domestic purposes. Regardless the level of human intervention, rabbits relate with nature. Like all living creatures, they like outdoor playtime.

Absent a safe area for your pet rabbit to run and play freely, you will need to enclose a space. As an alternative, some rabbit owners put their animals in a harness and use a leash. This is a topic where varying opinions and experiences exist.

Rabbit owners get a lot of attention walking harnessed rabbits in public places. Regardless how careful the owner or how good the harness, a rabbit in public is unnecessarily exposed to harsh sounds that humans cannot even hear. Also, car horns, barking dogs and other abrupt noises are very scary for these animals. Harnessed rabbits are often terror-stricken. Some have broken their partially-restrained spines trying to get away from whatever has frightened them.

It is important to minimize the stress to your pet by avoiding public areas with lots of traffic, population or noise. Such activities cause fear and anxiety. That would be the case with any prey animal, but is especially a problem for rabbits.

The best solution for outdoor play is an area which is relatively quiet, free of other animals and safely enclosed. Check out the area carefully and supervise your pet to ensure he cannot injure himself or escape.

Yard fencing often sits on the ground. This means your rabbit could dig a hole and quickly burrow under. If he winds up in the neighbor's yard, he might be attacked by a dog or other animal. Alternatively, he might just keep going, never to be seen again.

Other Options for Outdoor Play

Other options for outdoor play areas include building a permanent structure which is entirely fenced in, including on the top if he is to be in his play area unsupervised. Making sure the play area is fully enclosed will keep predators, such as birds, at bay.

Since rabbit are burrowing animals, make sure he cannot dig out. Avoid lining the ground with wire fencing. Placing them on top of such materials is not desirable and can harm fragile paws. Also, he his paws could get stuck, resulting in fractures and other injuries. If building a play area, consider lining the ground with indoor/outdoor carpeting or other rabbit-friendly material.

Another option is to enclose an area using pet playpen panels. Outdoor play spaces are easy to set up and take down. You can also use playpen materials to block off areas of the yard (or openings that expose the spaces under decks) where rabbits should not go.

Other outdoor concerns are birds or owls that prey on rabbits. Even neighborhood crows have been known to swoop down and attack rabbits. Foxes, racoons, skunks, nutria, feral cats and other animals are also a threat. Some of those animals can climb right up your fence and quickly drop into your yard. Unless an entirely closed play area is available, outdoor play time must be closely supervised.

Finally, your pet rabbit should not eat outside vegetation, including grass from the lawn that has been chemically treated or sprayed. Because he will want to eat plants in the yard, keep him away from anything that originates from bulbs and other poisonous-to-rabbit plants. They could cause serious illness and even be fatal.

Taking your rabbit outdoors even for 15 or 20 minutes will give him a nature-type experience and make him very happy.

Chapter Thirty
Outdoor Plants

Lila: Huma, can we eat that plant?
Me: I'm sorry, Lila. That plant is not safe.
Lila: Can we eat the apple tree leaves?
Me: Yes. You and Bandit may each have one.
Bandit: I can eat more than one.
Me: No, Bandit. That would not be good for your tummy.
Bandit: Okay, then I'll have one apple leaf and one raisin.
Me: No raisin today.
Bandit: Maybe I should just look for a raisin bush.
Me: That should keep you busy for a while.

Rabbit-safe versus poisonous plants are somewhat of a conundrum. For example, some veterinarians (who practice natural medicine with rabbits) might say that a small piece of oak leaf can help with parasite control in rabbits.

Other sources suggest that that oak can cause gastrointestinal problems in horses, so rabbits should also not consume them. Since rabbits are still largely understudied, information can vary greatly depending upon the source and context.

To further complicate plant-related research, not all plant varieties have the same levels of toxins. For example, there are different kinds of apple trees, strawberry plants, tomatoes and lettuces.

Since rabbits are strictly herbivores (vegan), they handle some plant consumption better than carnivorous animals. That does not mean they should eat plants that are known to adversely affect other animals.

Published information about plant toxicity is generally based on the most toxic plant in its category. This means that you might find a plant on the "do not feed your rabbit" list and find the same plant on the "okay to feed your rabbit" list.

Because of genetic modification of seeds and the development of new food varieties, it is becoming more difficult to determine which plant is safe and which is not. Since a rabbit's health can turn bad in a matter of hours, it is wise to err on the side of caution and limit access to outdoor plants.

A good rule of thumb is to keep your rabbit away from plants that originate from bulbs, genetically modified fruits and vegetables, and anything that is treated with chemicals. Some grasses are good for rabbits, while others are not. Some lettuces are good for rabbits (iceberg is not).

If rabbit-safe leaves, pine cones or small branches have been on the ground for a while, remember that parasites, bugs or worms might also be present. Wild rabbits can hop from one plant to another and get nature's medicine to solve resulting problems, but your pet does not have that option.

Any natural-for-rabbit foods such as twigs, leaves or pine cones should be cleaned before you give them to your pet. Diluting vinegar in water and using it as a wash is effective. Anything in a vinegar wash must be thoroughly rinsed and dried before feeding or storing.

When in Doubt, Limit Access

It is a good idea to feed your rabbit his favorite greens or other foods familiar to him prior to going outside. This will help deter him from nibbling on things he should not.

Even if your rabbit consumes plants that are perfectly safe, he could still have gastrointestinal problems because the flora in his gut is not accustomed to eating it.

The potential for your pet rabbit to eat a toxic plant is another reason to closely supervise him outdoors and limit his access to plants. If you can safely give your pet rabbit free run of your yard space, place barriers around plants and flowers that are questionable or off-limits.

If your pet rabbit does eat something that you believe could be toxic and he becomes ill (has changes in feces and urine or stops eating and drinking), call your veterinarian.

Jana Brock

Chapter Thirty-One
Bonus Bunny Stuff

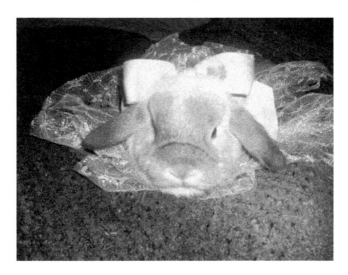

Lila: Huma, I am ready to go to the dress-up party.
Me: You look lovely. Is Bandit all dressed?
Lila: He doesn't want to go. He said he is too mature for parties.
Me: Hmmm. I suppose he won't want his party treat.
Lila: Yum! What kind of treat do we get?
Me: I am going to give you each some carrot peelings.
Bandit: (from across the room) I'm going!
Me: I thought you were too old for parties?
Bandit: Nonsense. I am just the right age.
Lila: You said you were far too mature.
Bandit: No one is too mature for parties, Lila.
Lila: Sometimes I can't believe I am bonded with you.
Bandit: Consider yourself fortunate. Lots of women would love to be in your spot.
Lila: Sometimes it takes a lot of patience to deal with you, Bandit.
Bandit: I'm worth it.

Happy Rabbit Tip

Digging is natural for rabbits. A safe way to encourage this behavior without risking damage to your home or furnishings is to make a simple digging box.

To replicate the box above, cut a hole in a plastic bin to make a doorway. Make sure the doorway is several inches from the floor so that the material is contained.

Apply heat to the edges of the plastic where you cut. Smooth edges will ensure your bunny does not get hurt jumping in and out. Since plastic will emit fumes when a flame or other heat is applied, do this in a well-ventilated area.

This digging box contains paper-based pellets which are rabbit-safe, but you can use other types of pellets, shredded paper or something else. When choosing digging material, make sure your rabbit will not eat it, use it for litter or harm his tender paws (shaved wood is not advisable because of splinters).

Sand is often used, though it packs into your rabbit's fur and sticks to delicate skin. Grooming increases, so sand particles are ingested which can cause problems for the digestive system. It can also accumulate in the lungs, eyes and ears. Over time, this could cause health problems for him and a costly veterinarian bill for you.

Bandit: Lila, there is a piece of hay in the water dish.
Lila: I saw that.
Bandit: Can you get it out?
Lila: I'm not the one who dropped it in there.
Bandit: But you always do the cleaning.
Lila: You need to learn to clean up your own messes.
Bandit: Woman, clean this dish at once!
Lila: What did you say to me?
Bandit: Uhhhh….

The Littles had a craft day. It was Bandit's idea. He really wanted to show Lila he is more mature than he was a few days ago when he stole her dinner. She thought it was a lovely gesture.

They worked together to make this beautiful sign for their new bunny enclosure. Bandit even offered to help me by chewing the strings that I used to hang it. Lila and I both said we were proud of him. He said that meant a lot.

Me: Good morning, Oates. How are you today?

Oates: Okay. I am just exploring your house.

Me: Don't you remember being here last time your humans went on vacation?

Oates: Yes, but things are different now.

Me: How so?

Oates: For starters, you have a new couch to chew on.

Me: That's right, we do have a new couch. Please do not chew on it, though.

Oates: Oh, sorry. I thought you bought it for us rabbits. It looks like a big chew toy.

Me: It does, yes. I forgot to cover it before your humans dropped you off.

Oates: You should do that soon.

Me. I'm on it.

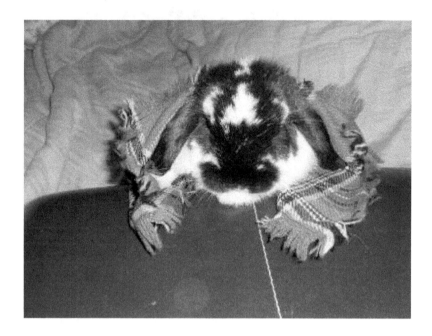

Bandit is disappointed. He had his heart set on a Superman costume. I explained to him that those types of clothes are too tight-fitting. Putting on a tight costume could cause an injury and I simply could not take that chance.

He was not happy, but he reluctantly agreed to wear a vintage blanket. He says that next time he goes to a dress-up party, he will hire a rabbit costume seamstress so he can dress up like Superman. I told him that would be okay.

Lila's Holiday Photo

Lila and Bandit were staring out the window talking about the strange white stuff falling from the sky. They begged and begged to go outside and investigate, but I explained to them that they were both small rabbits. That means they can get cold very quickly.

After some discussion, I finally agreed to let them see the snow. Lila requested a picture with she and Bandit's Christmas tree so I grabbed my camera and we went out to the yard.

After she posed for her holiday photo, I let her run around for about one minute before taking her back inside to warm up. I dried the snowflakes from her little paws, face and fur. She thanked me. She said it was a real thrill to be out in the snow for the first time ever.

As soon as she saw Bandit, she started chattering away, telling him about her outdoor snow adventure. He told me that he would like a turn, but he wanted his picture to be with Santa Claus.

Bandit's Holiday Photo

After Bandit finished listening to Lila's snow adventure story, I took him outdoors. He gave me strict instructions to take the picture while he was standing up tall. He said that it would make him look older and more mature.

After informing him that I got just the right photo, he got back down on all fours and started running and jumping around. He said he wanted to make lots of rabbit trails so everyone would know he had been there. He was sure that if any big rabbits came around, they would be jealous of his adventure.

The whole time I was carrying him back inside, he never stopped talking about his snow experience. He said he bets most house rabbits never get to have a snowy holiday picture taken with the REAL Santa Claus. He also told me he is certain Santa is bringing him a box of raisins for Christmas. He is planning to hide them so he can have treats whenever he wants.

Me: Lila, are you okay? You look a little wobbly.

Lila: I'm practicing my ice skating.

Me: Oh - I – uh. Hmmm.

Lila: It's a little slippery. Hard to keep from falling.

Me: You realize you're on a blanket, right?

Lila: Yes, but I'm using a mental technique to practice. That way, I'll be an expert when I get on the ice for real.

Me: I see. Where did you hear about this mental technique?

Lila: I read it in online.

Me: You read it – wait. How could you possibly –

Lila: I would really love to talk, Huma, but I need to concentrate.

Me: (scratching my head) Of course. I'll let you get back to it.

Jo: What's this enclosure for?
Me: It is a little space for your hay and food while you are visiting.
Jo: It doesn't have a door.
Me: Yes, but you wouldn't be able to get to your food if there was a door.
Jo: Oh, right. Well, it looks good.
Me: Thank you, Jo.
Jo: Nice floor. Real solid structure. Should work fine.
Me: I am glad you approve.

Lila: Oh, hey. You're new around here.

Oreo: Yup. My name is Oreo. I am a rescue.

Lila: Were you in a bad situation before?

Oreo: Yes. In fact, my prior owners dumped me on a street corner in the freezing cold and just drove away. Don't get me wrong, I was happy to get away from them, but I didn't know what to do. I was so cold and hungry.

Lila: That is terrible!

Oreo: Luckily, a nice human family found me and brought me here. Before the rescue, I didn't think any humans were nice.

Lila: Well, you will love it here. Our humans treat us very well. We have our own room, fresh hay, healthy food and clean water. Plus, we get to run in the halls and play in the yard. We even get treats.

Oreo: I must be in rabbit heaven.

Me: What are you doing in there, Bandit?
Bandit: Working on this digging-box. It is a very complicated project.
Me: I can come back later.
Bandit: Wait – maybe you can help me out.
Me: Sure. What can I do for you?
Bandit: Well, I could concentrate much better if I had a treat.
Me: I am guessing you want a raisin?
Bandit: It's like you can read my mind.
Me: Well, you and Lila don't get another treat until tomorrow.
Bandit: Bunstruction is very difficult without raisin energy.
Me: Raisin energy. Huh. Well, how about dandelion leaf energy instead?
Bandit: It's not as effective as raisin energy.
Me: It's your only option.
Bandit: I'll take it.

Happy Rabbit Tip

Rabbits can, and most often will, destroy books, DVD covers and everything else within their reach. Wooden book cases and shelves are especially attractive. Even if you clear the bottom shelf, house rabbits will nibble on the wood corners and other exposed edges.

Light-weight pet fencing is very useful for blocking off areas your rabbit should not access. Not only will you will protect him from eating things he should not, but you will preserve household items you care about.

I saw The Littles telling secrets so I knew they were up to something. I heard Bandit tell Lila they should sneak outside and play on the woodpile. He said he could hardly wait because there is so much to chew on!

I went into my bedroom and started reading a book. A few minutes later, I heard a noise. I tiptoed into the living room and peeked around the corner. I watched in amusement as they put their little paws up to the sliding glass door. They pushed and pushed but it would not budge.

After a few minutes, they gave up and flopped down on the floor. I heard Lila say, "Bandit, sneaking outside is too much work." Bandit quickly agreed and they both fell asleep.

Lila: Hey, Bandit. Doesn't your neck hurt in that position?
Bandit: No. I'm perfectly comfortable.
Lila: Okay. I just don't want you to get a sore neck.
Bandit: I lay like this all the time.
Lila: Every time I do that, I wake up with a crick.
Bandit: A crick – you mean water? Like a stream?
Lila: No. That's a creek.
Bandit: It doesn't make sense that I would fall asleep and wake up in a stream.
Lila: You wouldn't wake up in a creek. You would have a crick.
Bandit: This is too complicated. I'm going back to sleep.

Bandit: Are you trying to jump over the fence?
Oreo: Nah, I'm just sizing it up.
Bandit: It's too high.
Oreo: I think I could clear it.
Bandit: Oh, yeah? Let's see you jump over.
Oreo: I don't want to get in trouble.
Bandit: Huma won't mind. I already tried, though. It can't be done.
Oreo: Well, I am at least twice your size. I'm sure I could do it.
Bandit: I may be small, but I'm strong.
Oreo: I'm sure you are.
Bandit: I know karate.
Oreo: Huh. That's impressive.
Bandit: I can jump higher than most --
Oreo: Dude, give it a rest.

In Conclusion

There is a great deal more information about house rabbits beyond what is shared here. Even though studies specific to domesticated rabbits are still lacking, volumes of books could be written about what is presently known.

The more we communicate our personal knowledge and experience, the more we can clarify or correct historic misunderstandings. Sharing good information, even when challenged by others, ensures that we advance best care practices which help educate future rabbit owners.

When learning about responsible care, it is important to do your own research and realize that experienced rabbit owners sometimes disagree. Conflicting information exists regardless whether you are talking to a veterinarian, reading information on a rabbit organization website or talking to long-term rabbit owners.

Regardless how you resolve information discrepancies, remember what nature intended for these precious creatures. Do your best to learn best care practices. Responsible owners are always in demand because countless domesticated rabbits around the world are waiting to find their forever homes.

In conclusion, I would like to thank you for reading *Bunny Conversations*. I hope you found it informative and entertaining. Before you go, please enjoy the following excerpt from my upcoming book, *Rabbit Tails, The Adventures of Lila and Bandit*."

Be well,

Jana

Chapter One
In The Yard

"Bandit, come quick! There is a strange scent coming from underground. Maybe it's food."

"Be there in a minute," he yelled back from across the yard. He had some time before Lila would realize he hadn't rushed right over. Her harsh beginnings had left her with a delay, though he was careful to never mention it. Besides, he was on the scent of something, too.

Fervently digging, his white front paws scraped dirt from the ground. Little specs of Earth were flung onto his back, though most of it went under his abdomen in the direction of his hind legs. It then whizzed through the space beneath his tail and landed on a pile that was forming behind him.

Shortly, he uncovered several flower bulbs. "Oh, great," he said allowed. "Nothing to eat here."

He sat up on his hind legs to get a better view of Lila who was still across the yard, sniffing the ground. Just as he thought, she was still in the investigation stage and hadn't so much as scratched at the dirt.

Flopping down to rest, he glanced over at the small mound of dirt beside him. Even though flower bulbs are poisonous to rabbits, he was proud of his accomplishment. At least he'd dug up something.

He thought about rabbits in the wild. Though digging was part of their base nature, females were much more equipped for the task. Does preparing for litters instinctively scratch out holes while the bucks take more of a protector role.

Bandit was amazed thinking about rabbit holes. They become intricate networks of underground tunnels called warrens where does, bucks and kits live. Even though he lived indoors, he knew that rabbits in the wild needed protection from predators and harsh weather.

Rabbits in nature come above ground to forage, drink water and socialize. It was a lot of work. He knew that female rabbits were more motivated than him because digging was exhausting.

Legs stretched out behind his tail, front paws in a forward position and abdomen against the ground, he felt himself getting drowsy. He forgot about joining Lila as he drifted off to sleep. Eyes wide open, his nose stopped twitching. Sleep engulfed him and he began to dream.

The next thing he knew, he was back at the hole where he'd just found the bulbs. As he dug deeper, he felt his front paw scratch something solid. Not hard like a stone, but solid enough that his toenails could scratch the surface. Immediately, a sweet aroma reached his nose.

Unmistakably, carrot.

Bandit picked up his digging pace. His hard work and perseverance in yard digging was finally going to pay off. The smell got stronger. He could see the bright orange skin of the carrot – a welcome sight.

Using his teeth, he tried to grip the top of the tasty vegetable where the greens meet the flesh, but it would not budge. It was buried too deep. Together, he and Lila would have a better chance at getting that carrot out so he called her over.

Suddenly, he jolted awake. Sitting beside him was Lila who had a very disappointed look on her face. "Bandit, you never came to help me."

"Wait, what?" Bandit shook his head as he hopped onto his feet feeling somewhat confused. "I – uh – I found a carrot."

"A carrot?" Lila asked. "I don't smell anything but grass and dirt over here. And those noxious flower bulbs you unearthed."

Hesitantly, he looked over at his hole. Sure enough, two flower bulbs were visible near the bottom where he'd stopped digging earlier.

"Oh, right," he said. "Sorry, Lila. I fell asleep. I guess I was dreaming."

"It's okay," she said. She watched him walk his short, front paws out in front of him. He stretched and yawned, exposing his front teeth.

"How about you? Did you find anything?"

Lila shook her head as she scratched some dirt near Bandit's hole. "Nope. Nothing but bulbs over there."

"Dang," he said. "I'm really in the mood for a carrot. I can smell them in the raised garden bed."

Lila stopped digging and looked up at the tall wooden structure. She thought about their human ma (who they referred to as *Huma*) lifting her and Bandit up to the garden for summer pictures just a few days prior. After the photo shoot, they each got one carrot top as a treat.

Bandit looked at Lila with that "I-am-planning-something" expression that he so often got when trouble was afoot. "I wonder if Huma will give us a carrot treat if we ask nicely?"

He patiently watched her scratch around in the flowerbed. She didn't respond. The dirt beside his hole caught her attention. She started digging, then sniffing and digging again.

Bandit wasn't sure if Lila was just ignoring him or this was one of her delayed reactions. He decided it was important enough to repeat. "Lila, do you think Huma will give us a piece of carrot?"

"She's right over there. We could ask her."

He looked over at their human who was sitting on a lounge chair in the sun, book in one hand and ice water in the other. "Or we could just hop up to the garden and get our own carrots. That way, we won't have to disturb her."

Lila sat on her hind legs. Paws together, she gave them a firm shake to remove as much dirt as possible before touching her face. With one paw on either side of her nose, she made several forward sweeping motions before answering him.

"I don't think that is a good idea, Bandit. Huma told us we were never allowed in the gardens."

Bandit plopped down and made a "Humph" sound. "But she planted them especially for us, remember? She said they are organic."

Lila politely responded. "That is true, but she also made it clear that some things in the garden are not good for us. Potato greens, onions, leeks and other plants. Only she can pick from the garden."

Bandit looked dismayed and said under his breath, "So many rules."

Lila glanced across the yard just behind where Huma was sitting. "The raspberry leaves look good. We can eat those without asking. I'll go with you if you want some."

"I had raspberry leaves earlier. Besides, I have a hankering for carrots. Let's go ask."

The Littles hopped across the yard and stopped in front of the chair where their human was sitting. Standing on his hind legs, Bandit began to explain his position on eating carrots and why he and Lila deserve more treats.

Huma was amused, though she listened intently. She thanked him for the information and then talked about how sick rabbits can become when they do not eat properly. She said she would feel more comfortable giving them greens.

Bandit just stared at the garden with a disappointed look on his face. He then threw a sharp look at Lila for nodding, indicating her agreement with Huma's strict treat rules. Being the only survivor of a litter of sick kits had taught Lila an important lesson about rabbit health.

Huma decided to walk over to the garden. Her two small lops hopped closely behind her. She picked a carrot with a nice, full green top. Dividing the plentiful greens, she reached down and gave each rabbit half.

After the greens were eaten, Huma broke two small pieces from the carrot and handed them to the Littles. They usually did not get treats on Tuesdays, so the carrot pieces were an extra special treat. Still chewing, Bandit said that nothing was quite as good as fresh carrot on a warm summer's day.

Both rabbits joyfully sprinted back and forth across the yard, jumping and playing. They quickly tired and returned to the spot where Huma was standing. Tummies full, they followed her inside the house where they each flopped down for a long afternoon nap.

Jana Brock

About the Author

Jana Brock has worked in two professional careers over the past 30 years, specifically in law and emergency management. Her work experience and education have enhanced her research, writing and teaching skills.

Brock now dedicates her time to the world of domesticated rabbits. She has her own house rabbits and is also a bunny sitter. She has rehabilitated rescued rabbits that were abused or neglected by prior owners.

To continue documenting best care practices, Brock stays current with rabbit-related research. She is active in large online communities where people from all over the world share their knowledge and experience with other rabbit owners.

Jana Brock is presently finalizing *Rabbit Tails, The Adventures of Lila and Bandit*. This book is a lighthearted collection of short stories scheduled for release in 2017. She is also the author of *Just Keep Breathing, A Journey Through Grief and Recovery* (first and second editions).

More documentation of best care practices and other information relating to domesticated rabbits can be found by visiting *loveyourrabbit.com*.

www.ingramcontent.com/pod-product-compliance
Lightning Source LLC
La Vergne TN
LVHW020728291224
800112LV00032B/1109